# YOUR KNOWLEDGE H

- We will publish your bachelor's and master's thesis, essays and papers

- Your own eBook and book - sold worldwide in all relevant shops

- Earn money with each sale

## Upload your text at www.GRIN.com and publish for free

**Bibliographic information published by the German National Library:**

The German National Library lists this publication in the National Bibliography; detailed bibliographic data are available on the Internet at http://dnb.dnb.de .

**Imprint:**

Copyright © 2008 GRIN Verlag, Open Publishing GmbH
Print and binding: Books on Demand GmbH, Norderstedt Germany
ISBN: 978-3-668-04972-7

**This book at GRIN:**

http://www.grin.com/en/e-book/302933/long-term-archival-of-encrypted-records

**Angel Rivera**

# Long-Term Archival of Encrypted Records

GRIN Publishing

**GRIN - Your knowledge has value**

Since its foundation in 1998, GRIN has specialized in publishing academic texts by students, college teachers and other academics as e-book and printed book. The website www.grin.com is an ideal platform for presenting term papers, final papers, scientific essays, dissertations and specialist books.

**Visit us on the internet:**

http://www.grin.com/

http://www.facebook.com/grincom

http://www.twitter.com/grin_com

A STUDY OF THE USE OF ENCRYPTION TO PROTECT THE CONFIDENTIALITY

AND INTEGRITY OF ELECTRONIC RECORDS AS IT RELATES TO RETRIEVING

THOSE RECORDS FROM LONG TERM ARCHIVAL STORAGE

A DIRECTED RESEARCH PROJECT SUBMITTED TO THE FACULTY OF THE

GRADUATE SCHOOL OF COMPUTER INFORMATION SYSTEMS IN CANDIDACY

FOR THE DEGREE OF MASTER OF SCIENCE

BY ANGEL L. RIVERA

ARLINGTON CAMPUS

STRAYER UNIVERSITY

JUNE, 2008

Use of Encryption to Protect the Confidentiality and Integrity of Electronic Records

Abstract

Introduction

Encryption has proven itself throughout history as a very effective tool in providing for the confidentiality and integrity of information. Recent advances in encryption algorithms have made deciphering an encrypted piece of information without the encryption key practically impossible. According to the National Institute of Standards and Technology (NIST), "Assuming that one could build a machine that could recover a DES key in a second (i.e., try 255 keys per second), then it would take that machine approximately 149 thousand-billion (149 trillion) years to crack a 128-bit AES key. To put that into perspective, the universe is believed to be less than 20 billion years old" (NIST, 2008). While this sounds impressive it also posses the critical question of what happens when the encryption key is lost? Will the information be lost forever? This research study, attempts to answer the main question of what would be the impact of encryption on long term electronic records retention and retrieval? Since these records have been archived for many years, the potential for loosing the encryption key, the encryption software, or the link between the key and specific records increases considerably.

To complete this research an extensive literature search was conducted, followed by interviews with practitioners, researchers and technology implementers. Additionally, the author built a proof-of- concept of a virtual computer.

Main research was focused on issues associated with long term archival of electronic records, encryption, and virtual machine software.

Summary

In terms of archival records, the research focused on prior and current work by libraries and researchers dealing with the preservation of digital records. This part of the research identified problems and solutions associated with old media and the lack of available software to interpret electronic records, as well as the lack of hardware needed to read some of the media. Only one authoritative source was identified in terms of encryption and archival records, that being the National Archives and Records Administration (NARA). However, encryption in this case was only related to the use of encryption for digital signatures not the encryption of records. Such authoritative source was not discounted all together because many of NARA's recommendations could apply to the long term archival of encrypted records.

For encryption, the research focused on current encryption technologies and guidance with an emphasis on key management. Key management was selected due to the fact that it addresses specific areas of interest including key escrow and key recovery. Substantial information was available in this area; however, some of the guidance was in conflict with the storage of encrypted records for long periods of time. This is because encryption is recommended for shorter periods of time unless the encryption keys are changed frequently. For example, the current NIST guidance is to keep encryption keys for a maximum of three years while government requirements in many cases require long term archival of official records for 7-10 years.

The last research chapter is focused on virtual machine software as a technology that has recently matured to a level that is being adopted by all types of organizations and as a technology that has the potential to address some of the issues associated with the long term archival of electronic records. Virtual machines (VMs) can be used for the purposes of archiving the operating system, the encryption software, and for the purposes of emulating hardware and media that might soon be extinct. In essence, VMs allow you to decouple the operating system (OS) and the software from the media and the hardware by emulating a complete computing environment. As a proof of concept the author was able to build a Microsoft Windows 95 virtual machine, with encryption software, and floppy disk/drive emulation. This VM was saved to a DVD, which can last more than ten years. Additionally, it contains everything needed to restore a computer and software that is over ten years old on any x86 platform.

Conclusion

Strong evidence exists in terms of recent data leaks as well as multiple regulatory mandates that points to the increased use of encryption. Organizations that process and maintain personal information are particularly rushing to encrypt all such data. From the author's point of view this rush is being propelled by the potential for huge financial losses rather than the concern for the individual whose personal information might be compromised. The risks associated with stealing personal information are magnified more than ever since identity theft became such a lucrative market for criminals. Encryption is a double edge sword that should be used with caution. This powerful technology can be used to protect sensitive information from criminals by making it unreadable; however, improperly implementing this technology can also render the information unreadable to the organization, resulting in a self-inflicted denial-of-service attack.

This paper intensifies the risks associated with encryption and with the long-term archival of electronic records. The paper also identified several pieces of guidance and standards that can be used to reduce those risks; which were scattered all over the place rather than a single location. Each guidance, or standard, addresses only part of a possible solution.

Virtual machines are a viable option to address the issue of older hardware, older operating systems, and encryption software. However, a conscious decision must be made now to preserve older hardware and older operating systems before running the risk of losing them forever.

More research is needed to put all the pieces together into a comprehensive strategy for encrypted records retention. As a starting point, the strategy should consider prior work identified in this research paper. The lack of such a comprehensive strategy can lead to the loss of valuable information, maybe forever, and the consequences can be devastating.

Acknowledgments

I would like to take this opportunity to thank my family, my wife in particular since she had to keep the household going while I studied many weekends. To my daughter and my wife thanks for your patience reading my drafts and providing me with constructive feedback, I know that for non-technical people, encryption and virtual machines can be quite a dry subject. I can only hope that my hard work and dedication in some way has inspired my two college age children and that they take it as an example on how to accomplish great things even if it is short steps at a time.

To my employer, The Mitre Corporation, my hat is off to you for paying for this degree and providing an environment that allowed me access to multiple experts in the field; experts that served as a sounding board and contributed to several interviews. Many thanks to J.P for taking the time to educate me on virtual machine software, a completely new field for me. To M.R., who I consider an authoritative source on encryption, many thanks for sharing your expertise and real life experience. To S.B., published author and recognized security subject matter expert, thank you for pointing me in the right direction and for taking the time to validate information from one of your published books.

I also must recognized industry experts, C.L. and S.B., for taking time out of their busy schedule and talking to me about a topic that many organizations consider sensitive. I was unsuccessful in getting interviews with law-enforcement personnel because they are not allowed to talk about fraud and techniques to detect fraud or to provide good examples of when electronic records were not accessible. You both provided me excellent examples and perspectives that made this research paper that much stronger.

Last but not least, thanks to the IRS and two of their employees, G.J. and B.B., for sharing with me their lessons learned on implementing encryption and virtual machine software for such a large organization. I could not have asked for a better real-world example.

To Strayer University and all the professors that teach on-line courses, I could not have done this without you. As a professional that has no control over his schedule and travels quite a bit, I would not have completed my master's degree if I had to attend classroom classes. I encourage you to continue offering courses online; it makes the world of difference to students like myself.

Table of Contents

List of Tables and Figures

CHAPTER 1: Introduction

Context of the Problem

The government as well as corporate America has regulatory requirements to keep copies of electronic records for several years in case they need to be retrieved for legal or historical purposes. Just recently e-mail was added to the types of electronic records that organizations must back up and keep copies of for long periods of time. Regulations like the Privacy Act of 1974, the Sarbanes-Oxley Act of 2002 (for financial records), and the Health Insurance Portability and Accountability Act of 1996 require the protection of electronic records. One of the mandated technologies used to protect these records is encryption. When these encrypted records are archived, it might be difficult or impossible to retrieve them because the codes used for encryption might not be available.

Encryption can be traced back to the Spartans, a Greek society dating back to 400 BC. This military based society used encryption to encipher messages. According to Shawn Harris in his All-in-One CISSP book, he explains how the Spartans would write a message on a sheet of papyrus that was wrapped around a wooden stick, which was then delivered without the wooden stick to the recipient (Harris, 2008). The recipient would then wrap the papyrus around another wooden stick of the same circumference. This technique is referred to as the scytale cipher. This type of encryption uses transposition. This is what a scytale looks like:

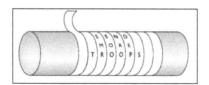

**Figure 1.1 - Scytale**
**Source - CISSP All-in-One Guide by Shawn Harris**

The person writing the message would wrap the paper around the baton and write the message. The message would then be sent via messenger without the baton. The recipient of the message would have a baton with the same circumference. When this person received the roll of paper he would wrap it around the baton and read it. If the messenger were intercepted by the enemy all they would get would be a roll of paper with gibberish. The baton is the key to enciphering and deciphering the message. More on encryption keys later.

In its simplest form, encryption is the process of transforming plain text into cipher text. Decryption is the process of transforming that cipher text into plain text again. The main use of encryption is to protect or provide for the confidentiality of data. However, today encryption is also used to provide for advanced authentication (e.g. smart cards, SecureID Tokens, X.509 certificates) and digital signatures. In the world of spies and the military, you can say it is used to provide secrecy of data and messages. To transform the data back and forth you need a process, also know as an algorithm, and, as part of that algorithm, you will need a key or code to be able to encrypt and decrypt the text. An encryption key is analogous to the combination you would need to open a safe. Most data encryption algorithms in use today use the same key to encrypt and decrypt the data. These algorithms are called symmetric key algorithms. Anyone with the key would be able to decrypt the cipher text, therefore, the need to protect that key and make it secret.

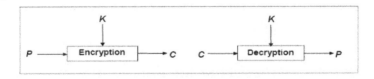

**Figure 1.2 - Encryption and Decryption**
**Source - National Institute of Standards Special Publication 800-21 – Guideline for Implementing Cryptography in the Federal Government**

"Figure 1.2 depicts the encryption and decryption processes. The plaintext (P) and a key (K) are used by the encryption process to produce the ciphertext (C). To decrypt, the ciphertext (C) and the same key (K) are used by the decryption process to recover the plaintext (P)" (NIST, 2005, p. 23).

Another historical example of encryption and encryption algorithms that is well known is the Caesar's cipher, used by Julius Caesar around 44 BC to exchange messages between him and his generals. Caesar's cipher just uses substitution of letters within the alphabet. For example, if you substitute every three letters, the letter "a" would become the letter "d" and the letter "b" would become the letter "e" and so forth. In this case the encryption key would be 3 and it could be changed frequently to make it harder to break the cipher text.

As you can imagine, the invention of the computer had a big impact on encryption, and IBM, being at the forefront of computers, created an encryption algorithm that remained unbroken for many years. This algorithm became the Data Encryption Standard (DES) and it was adopted by the federal government in 1977. A slight modification of this standard known as the Triple Data Encryption Algorithm (TDEA) is still approved for use today. What made this standard unique was that it was a published standard as opposed to secret algorithms used by intelligence agencies. This means the algorithm is available to anyone in the world; so code-breakers could get a copy and try to break it. The algorithm was so good that it remained unbroken until 1997 when "Tens of thousands of computers, all across the U.S. and Canada, linked together via the Internet in an unprecedented cooperative supercomputing effort to decrypt a message encoded with the government-endorsed Data Encryption Standard (DES)" (Purdue University, 1997, p. 30). The project is known as the Deschall Project and it was led by Rocke Verser from Loveland, Colorado.

3

Encryption was mostly used to secure communication messages between two parties. Examples of these included exchanging secret messages during wartime and securing financial transaction messages like electronic funds transfers. To secure electronic messages the encryption key was only good for a limited time. Two reasons for this were that you only needed it to send and receive the message; once the message had been deciphered you were done with the key. If you kept the same key for a long time there would be a pretty good chance more people would know the key. Additionally, an enemy trying to crack the code would have a better chance of cracking the code by trying all possible keys. Once cracked, the enemy would have access to all the messages; therefore, communicating parties would need to change keys frequently. As indicated before, not only did computers have a big impact on encryption but it also provided the same powerful tool to code breakers. This required even more frequent changes for the encryption keys. Frequent key changes pose an expensive and significant challenge to the communicating parties because both parties need the same key (shared secret). Imagine what that would mean in the case of the Spartans. Every time I changed the scytale I would have to send a messenger with the new scytale, hope it was not intercepted, and then send messages using this new scytale.

To address the challenge of key exchanges between communicating parties, public key encryption was invented. Public key encryption is also called asymmetric encryption because it uses two different encryption keys. "The first invention of asymmetric key algorithms was by James H. Ellis, Clifford Cocks, and Malcolm Williamson at GCHQ in the UK in the early 1970s; these inventions were what later became known as Diffie-Hellman key exchange, and a special case of RSA. This fact was kept secret until 1997" (Public Key Cryptography, 2006, para. 11).

"Public key cryptography is an encryption scheme that allows private communications to take place without prior existence of a shared secret" (Tulloch, 2003). With this type of encryption every user gets a pair of keys. One of them is called a public key and it can be shared with everyone. The second key is called a private key and it is only known and possessed by the user. One key is used to encrypt and the other one is used to decrypt. If user A wants to send an encrypted message to user B he will obtain user B's public key and encrypt the message. User B will use his private key to decrypt the message. The process is reversed if user B wants to send user A an encrypted message. Public key cryptography is the most common method used today to exchange secure e-mail messages. User A can send user B his public key via e-mail and vice versa. Once this is done both users can exchange email securely.

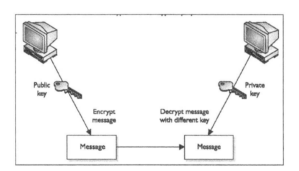

**Figure 1.3 - Asymmetric Cryptosystem**
**Source -CISSP All-in-One Guide by Shawn Harris**

Public key cryptography also provided for two additional features: The ability to sign a message (ensuring it was sent from the sender) and to guarantee that the message was not tampered with. The way this works is opposite to encrypting the message. User A can sign a message with his private key and attach the signature to the message. The message need not be encrypted. When user B receives the message from user A, he can verify the signature by

5

applying user A's public key. The use of encryption for digitally signing messages has been extended to digitally signing documents like contracts, therefore, replacing the need for a hand written signature. However, to make this electronic signature legally valid, both parties need to demonstrate that the private keys were indeed private and that those keys were obtained through secure channels and after strong personal identity verification. Digitally signed documents have some of the same challenges as encrypted records because in most cases these legally binding documents will be stored sometimes permanently, meaning forever. To validate the authenticity of the signature would require access to the public and private keys used to sign and validate the document.

Today, encryption is used for more than electronic messages. It is used to store sensitive information on electronic devices such as laptops. Therefore, if the laptop was lost or stolen, the data would remain secret. If the Department of Veterans Affairs employee had encrypted the data on his laptop, then the recent theft of his laptop with personal information on 26 million veterans would have been no big deal (VA Watchdog, 2006).

Encrypting data stored on computers has some unique challenges when it comes to encryption keys. The keys are normally used for long periods of time and the organization should retain copies of the keys in the event that the employee leaves. If each employee has a different encryption key, which is usually the case, then the organization needs to keep track of all these keys. The problem is further complicated when records are stored for long term archival purposes; which is the main focus of this research paper.

So far we have identified two reasons for storage and tracking of encryption keys: One is to ensure records that have been encrypted by an employee can be decrypted by the organization and the other one is to validate digital signatures sometime in the future. You can imagine the

6

amount of resources required to keep track of these keys for thousands of users and having to maintain the link between those users as well as the billions of electronic records. To make this process more manageable and to provide for the legal requirements of digital signatures a new concept emerged called public key infrastructure or PKI.

At its core, PKI is several technologies and processes used to authenticate entities through the use of public key encryption. Most implementations of PKI provide for storing of encryption keys, public keys, and digital certificates. "A digital certificate is encrypted information that guarantees that an encryption key belongs to a user" (Tulloch, 2003, 7). To be valid and to be accepted/trusted by external parties, digital certificates are issued by a trusted Certificate Authority (CA). A well-known CA is Verisign and a common implementation of PKI is Secure Sockets Layer (SSL) used on the Internet to secure communications between the client and secure web servers. When you visit a website and it says it is secure it means that it is using SSL and that it obtained the SSL certificate from a trusted CA like Verisign.

Within organizations, PKI is usually deployed for encryption, digital signature, and strong authentication. Strong authentication in this case means something stronger than passwords. Since it uses encryption, it is virtually impossible to crack. Additionally, digital certificates used for authentication remain in the possession of the user, making it hard to steal or share. For encryption and digital signature, PKI not only provides for making backup copies of user encryption keys, but also for making copies and publishing user's public keys. The PKI does not keep copies of private keys used for digital signatures because that would violate the legality of a digital signature. The private keys must only be issued to the individual and remain in their possession. Otherwise, the organization or someone with access to the computer that stores the keys could impersonate the user. In essence, PKI has solved the problem of storing encryption keys for cases when the user leaves the organization. In terms of accessing encrypted records that have been stored off-site for long term record retention you would think it would be easy to just go back to the PKI and retrieve keys, however, several factors complicate this mater. PKI, again for legal reasons, only issues digital certificates that are valid for a limited amount of time – usually 3-5 years. Therefore the PKI will now need to keep track of copies of new and old certificates as they are issued to the user. PKI as it currently exists is also technology and vendor dependent. What happens if the vendor goes out of business? Will I have to keep a copy of the PKI technology, which is quite expensive, to be able to retrieve encryption keys five or ten years from now?

To be compatible and interoperable across many computing platforms, encryption technology vendors have adopted industry standards. These standards include standards published by the National Institute of Standards and Technology (NIST), the International Standards Organization (ISO), and the American National Standards Institute (ANSI), to name a few. However, these standards come with a variety of implementation options, which leads to incompatible systems. A simple standard implementation example would be the strength of the encryption algorithm. Some vendors use codes that are 128 bits long and others use codes that are 256 bits long.

There are several government laws and regulations that call for the long term storage of electronic records. In publicly held companies there are also legal requirements to keep records for a long time. This might include financial records, external audits, minutes from board of director's meetings, etc. Health and insurance companies also have requirements for long term record retention. In the Federal Government, the agency responsible for providing guidance and for storing certain records for archival purposes is the National Archives and Records

Administration. As indicated in the beginning of this chapter, several government regulations require the protection of electronic records and some even require encryption as the technology to protect those records.

A key question for organizations is what happens when the records that need to be retrieved from long term storage are encrypted. The organization would need the encryption key to decrypt them but that key might not be available. The user might still be working for the organization but his key might have changed several times. Does the user have a copy of the code that he used 4 years ago when the organization's policy requires that he change his code every other year? Worst yet, did the user leave or pass away. Let's take a best-case scenario and assume we have a copy of the secret code. Will you need the same software the user used when they initially encrypted the data so it will understand the code to decrypt it? Even if the key is available the organization might need the same software the user used when they initially encrypted the data so it will understand the code to decrypt it.

Concerns about the preservation of digital documents go way back into the late 1980's and early 1990s. "A 1990 House of Representatives report cited a number of cases of significant digital records that had already been lost or were in serious jeopardy of being lost" (Rothenberg, 1999). For example, what would be the benefit of preserving a document encrypted in a 1995 version of Pretty Good Privacy (PGP) format if I don't have the PGP software to read it? Add to that the fact that document might be in WordPerfect format and I might not have WordPerfect software to read it even after I decrypt it. Several papers have been published on the preservation of digital information but one area of particular interest to this researcher is the use of virtual computing machines (VCM) as a way of preserving not only the digital information but the operating system and the software needed to properly interpret such information. VCM systems have been in use for quite a while, especially in the mainframe world where several

instantiations of a mainframe could be running on one piece of hardware as long as each

mainframe was running on its own logical partition. In the workstation and server environment,

the use of VCM software, like VMware, has been increasing steadily. In addition, CPU

manufacturers like Intel and AMD have started to build features into their platforms that support

virtual computing machines.

The purpose of this research is to address some of these issues in detail as well as identify

processes and technologies that will help organizations prepare for the long term archival and

retrieval of encrypted electronic records.


## Statement of the Problem

Encryption is increasingly being used to protect the confidentiality of data while stored in

electronic from. Encryption is the process of making information unreadable to any observer

with the exception of the person that holds the secret code that can decrypt the information.

However, the loss of the secret code could result in the loss of access to encrypted records.

The government, as well as corporate America, has some regulatory requirements to keep

copies of electronic records for several years in case they need to be retrieved for legal or

historical purposes. What happens when the records that need to be retrieved from long term

storage are encrypted? You would need that secret code to decrypt them but where is that code?

Will you need the same software the user used when they initially encrypted the data so it will

understand the code to decrypt it? The capability of being able to retrieve encrypted records from

long term storage and retrieval is an important topic of concern.

Concerns about the preservation of digital documents go way back into the late 1980s and early 1990s. Several strategies have been developed by private and public organizations and several papers have been published in industry journals and periodicals. However, a recent review of available literature shows little to no guidance when it comes to encrypted electronic records. One area of particular interest to this researcher is the use of virtual computing machines (VCM) as a way of preserving not only the digital information but also the operating system and the software needed to properly interpret such information.

The main problem is the lack of guidance and technologies that will allow for the retrieval of encrypted records that have been stored for archival purposes. Retrieval includes the capability to read/interpret/view the information.

## Main Research Question

What is the impact of encryption on long term electronic records retention and retrieval?

## Specific Research Sub-Questions

1. What are some of the possible consequences for organization that are unable to retrieve encrypted records from long term storage?

2. Can encryption codes be stored for long periods of time and be linked to the encrypted records?

3. What is the current state of Virtual Computing Machines software and can this software be used to address some of the problems associated with long term archival and retrieval of encrypted records?

11

Significance of the Study

Not being able to retrieve records from long term storage can have serious consequences. From an academic and research point of view, historical and statistical information as well as research information might be lost. This would require students and researchers to start from ground zero; recreating prior research or attempting to put together historical data from other sources. Loss of research data in the medical community and the pharmaceutical industry can have catastrophic consequences and place both communities years behind. From a legal liability perspective, companies could face serious lawsuits when encrypted data becomes inaccessible. Think about the consequences of being subpoenaed for something like e-mail records and not being able to produce them because they were encrypted. Organizations that deploy encryption or condone the use of encryption, but fail to provide for key escrow and back up and provide for the capability to retrieve encrypted electronic records, could be accused of criminal negligence. From a disaster recovery point of view, organizations would fail to restore electronic records if they cannot decrypt them.

Encryption is far too useful a technology to protect confidentiality and integrity of electronic records. Think about the recent case dealing with the theft of personal information for 26 million veterans. Encryption would have prevented the disclosure of that information not the theft. However, such a powerful technology comes with some responsibilities and organizations need to not only accept such responsibilities but also prepare for unexpected events and scenarios that will require the retrieval of encrypted electronic records from storage.

The problem with long term storage of encrypted records is compounded by the problem of long term storage of any electronic record that depends on an application for interpretation. As a result, the significance of this study is broken into two parts. First, the researcher will

12

address the issue of long term storage of encryption keys and their association to specific

electronic records. Second, the researcher will address the issue of long term storage of the

application(s) needed to decrypt electronic records. On the second part, the researcher will focus

on one specific technology: Virtual Computing Machines (VCM).


Research Design and Methodology

For this study the researcher will use interviews, content analysis, and a computer lab

proof-of-concept. Data will be collected and analyzed from computer periodicals, Internet

websites, information security books and articles. A primary source of data will be official

guidance and standards provided by the National Institute of Standards and Technology (NIST)

and the National Archives and Records Administration (NARA). The data that will be

collected/analyzed and it will be focused on two interrelated topics: Encryption and electronic

records long term archival. Interviews will be conducted with encryption and VCM subject

matter experts as well as government employees/contractors responsible for records management

and implementation of encryption technologies.

While NARA has published guidance on retention of records that have been digitally

signed and the requirement to prove the validity of the signature over a long period of time,

preliminary research has found that not many government agencies have been able to implement

such guidance.

Approaches to encryption key backup and recovery will be explored. Evaluation software

will also be obtained from VCM and file encryption vendors.

The researcher plans to set up the following test scenario to demonstrate that creating a virtual machine in software and then saving it as a back up with its encryption keys would be one way of addressing long term archival of encrypted files: The following steps were taken:

1- Set up a Windows 95 VMware instantiation in an older computer.

2- Load an old version of Pretty Good Privacy (PGP) encryption software.

3- Load an older version of Microsoft Word.

3- Encrypt a couple of files with PGP and Microsoft Word.

4- Save the Image

5- Reload the image on a new PC running Windows Vista.

6- Run PGP and Decrypt the files.


The purpose of this exercise is to demonstrate that an environment that is 14+ years old can be easily recreated today. Most government regulations require 5-10 years for availability of the information.

The researcher will also attempt to read the files with the latest version of PGP and Microsoft Word to determine if there are any problems decrypting the files. The purpose of this second step is to determine more or less how far vendors maintain backward compatibility.


Organization of the Study

Chapter One: This chapter provides a detail description of symmetric and asymmetric encryption in an attempt to bring about the complexities of such technology. This technology is currently being used to protect the confidentiality of data while stored in electronic form. Encryption has many uses besides protecting the confidentiality of records. Among these include

14

the protection of information while in transit, digital signatures, provision for non repudiation, and to guarantee the integrity of the electronic records and messages, as well as a form of strong authentication to computer systems. The focus of this study is limited to storage of electronic records that have been encrypted.

This chapter also provides a description of PKI, which is a set of technologies and processes that can assist in the recovery of encrypted electronic records. The chapter includes a brief mention of laws and regulations that mandate long term storage of electronic records and encryption in order to create awareness of the impact of encryption on long term electronic records retention and retrieval. The chapter identifies the interdependencies of encryption standards, encryption keys, and electronic records. It brings to light the lack of guidance and technology that will allow for the retrieval of encrypted records that have been stored for archival purposes.

Chapter Two: This chapter will include a summary of the literature reviewed by the researcher. Key documents for review include NIST standards for data encryption and key management, as well as NARA guidance for long-term storage of electronic records and digital signatures. Several published articles and white papers in the area of preservation of digital information will also be reviewed. Main sources include the Internet and the Association for Computing Machinery.

Chapter Three: This chapter will attempt to answer the following question: What are some of the possible consequences for organization that are unable to retrieve encrypted records from long term storage? The researcher will provide several hypothetical scenarios and cover implications related to loss of research data, data need for internal and external fraud investigations, as well as legal implications. The researcher will attempt to interview law enforcement personnel or fraud investigators that might be impacted by the unavailability of critical data.

Chapter Four: This chapter will attempt to answer the following question: Can encryption codes be stored for long periods of time and be linked to the encrypted records? The focus of this chapter will be key management strategies and policies, with a tie into backup and recovery of key infrastructure components or applications. The goal is to lead the reader into one possible comprehensive strategy of backing up complete images via VCMs that can be restored 10+ years from today and maybe longer.

Chapter Five: This chapter will cover the current state of Virtual Computing Machines software and evaluate this software to determine if it can be used to address some of the problems associated with long term retrieval of encrypted records. The focus will be on the top 2-3 VCM vendors. This chapter will also include a description of the lab work and the results of building a prototype for demonstration purposes.

Chapter Six: This chapter will provide a summary of the research project and provide the authors conclusions. The goal is to be able to convince the readers of the serious implications associated with long term storage of encrypted records. The goal is not to discourage the use of such technology but to promote the responsible use of encryption.

CHAPTER 2: Literature Review


Recent legislation as well as several well-publicized incidents have propelled and expedited the encryption of electronic records. Encryption is a proven technology that can safeguard the confidentiality of data stored for archival purposes. However, as indicated by the Office of Management and Budget (OMB) back in 2001 "encryption of agency data also presents risks to the availability of information needed by the agency to reliably meet its mission. Specifically, without access to cryptographic keys needed to decrypt information, the agency risks losing access to its valuable information" (OMB, 2001). The agency will not only need access to the encryption keys but to the software used to encrypt the data. Access to such software becomes problematic when several years have passed by. During this timeframe many factors can affect the availability of such software. These might include changes in operating systems, computing hardware, and the probability that the software vendor might go out of business.

Libraries and government agencies responsible for archival of government information (e.g., The National Archives and Records Administration) have been working on the preservation of digital information for a while. They too have identified a dependency between digital records and the software needed to interpret them. One approach identified by researchers that merits further consideration is the use of virtual computing machines that could recreate the software and hardware environment now and in the future.

This paper deals with the numerous issues associated with long term archival of encrypted digital records. Consequently, the literature identified for this research can be divided into three main areas:

- Encryption

- Long-term archival and preservation of digital information

- Virtual computing software

Encryption

In March 2005, the Enterprise Strategy Group (ESG) conducted a study entitled

"Information at Risk: The State of Backup Encryption" (Whitehouse, 2006). In that study ESG

raises the issue that there is quite a bit of sensitive data being stored on backup tapes,

nevertheless, users are leery of using encryption for many reasons. While cost and performance

remained the main deterrents, the study contains other factors related to this research paper

including issues with key management and disaster recovery.

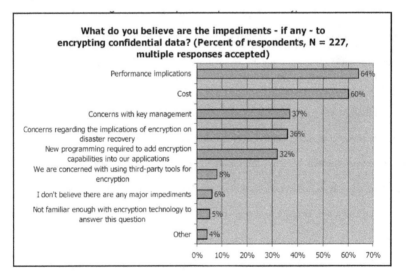

**Figure 2.1 – Perceptions of Impediments to Encryption**
**Source – ESG Snapshot Study Information at Risk: The State of Backup Encryption**

In 2007, PGP Corporation sponsored a study by The Ponemon Institute on the United States Encryption trends. PGP Corporation is well known for its encryption product Pretty Good Privacy (PGP). The public domain version of PGP has become a de facto encryption standard on the Internet. One of the reasons why PGP sponsored the research was because The Ponemon Institute had been conducting extensive research in the area of data breaches. According to a study by the institute in 2006, "the average cost of a data breach per record compromised grew 30 percent, averaging a total of $4.8 million per breach" (Ponemon Institute, 2007). One method organizations are using to reduce or eliminate data breaches is to encrypt sensitive information. The study sponsored by PGP focused on the current encryption trends and tried to answer the following questions:

- Why are enterprises using encryption?
- What encryption applications are in use?
- How are organizations planning for use?
- What type of encryption approach do they prefer?

The study was done via survey to 768 IT and business managers in the U.S. This encryption trends study was also trying to determine if organizations were taking a strategic approach to encryption. As encryption and encryption technologies are explained in this paper, the reader will realize how complex encryption can be and how important it is to have a strategy that addresses encryption, key management, archival of encrypted data and their associated encryption keys, applications that encrypt data or applications that use encryption service, and restoration/recovery of encrypted data in the event of a disaster. A poorly implemented strategy or having no strategy can easily turn into a self-inflicted denial-of-service when the organization is unable to decrypt data. This is because they do not have the encryption keys used to encrypt or because they are unable to associate keys with applications and encrypted information.

19

Among the top reasons organizations are deciding to encrypt data are mitigating data breaches and compliance with privacy or other security related regulations.

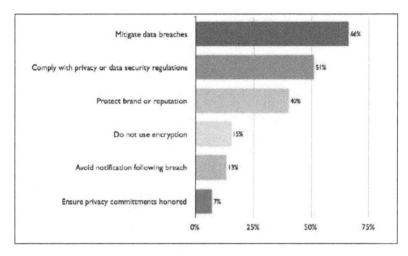

**Figure 2.2 – Top reasons why organizations encrypt sensitive/confidential data**
**Source – PGP/2007 Annual Study: U.S. Enterprise Encryption Trends**

The study identified that four major applications are using encryption, with laptop encryption being the most common. For the purposes of this research project, e-mail encryption, and backup encryption are areas of interest.

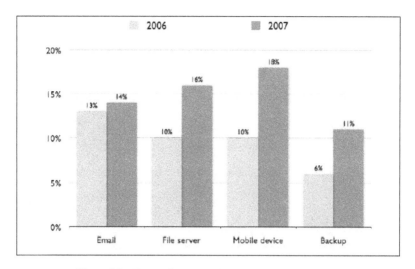

**Figure 2.3 – Enterprise encryption use by application type**
**Source – PGP/2007 Annual Study: U.S. Enterprise Encryption Trends**

One more aspect worth mentioning about the PGP study was the emphasis on using an
encryption platform to deploy encryption throughout the enterprise. This is important because in
the absence of such platform, the company runs the risk of purchasing several encryption
technologies, supported by separate vendors, all of which would raise deployment and
maintenance costs and increase the risk of mismanaging encryption keys. A platform-based
approach would centralize all encryption functions and manage them centrally. Encryption key
management policies can be enforced from a central location. In chapter one we described a
Public Key Infrastructure (PKI). A PKI would be a foundational building block for an
encryption platform.

In 1987 Congress enacted Public Law 100-235, which is also known as the Computer

Security Act of 1987. In this Act, the National Institute of Standards and Technology was given

the "responsibility within the Federal Government for developing technical, management,

physical and administrative standards and guidelines for the cost-effective security and privacy

of sensitive information in Federal computers" (Computer Security Act, 1987). This Act has

now been superseded by the Federal Information Security Management Act (FISMA) of 2002 at

which time NIST responsibilities were reconfirmed and expanded. NIST publishes security

standards in two forms: Federal Information Publishing Standards, commonly known as FIPS,

and NIST Special Publications also known as NIST SPs. FIPS have always been mandatory for

federal agencies. SPs started as guidance but FISMA and several Office of Management and

Budget (OMB) mandates have made them mandatory. For this paper the author was most

interested in encryption standards. A thorough understanding of the interworking of encryption

is important in order to start the analysis of specific research sub-question one: What are some of

the possible consequences for organizations that are unable to retrieve encrypted records from

long term storage?

The first encryption standard published by NIST was FIPS PUB 46 "Data Encryption

Standard" published in 1977. As explained in chapter one, this standard, which is based on

IBM's Lucifer cipher, remained unbroken until 1997. Today a version of DES called Triple

DES, or TDES, is still approved for the protection of sensitive data; however, DES was replaced

in 2001 by FIPS 197 "Advanced Encryption Standard (AES)" (NIST, 2001). The following

figure shows how complex the DES encryption standard is. The standard used 56 bit encryption

keys. Encryption keys of this length have become obsolete and replaced with algorithms that use

128 or 256 bit keys. To encrypt data, every 8 bits went through 16 rounds of encryption.

According to Shon Harris, author of the All-In-One Computer Information System Security

Professional (CISSP) Exam Guide, DES is the most common encryption algorithm in the world

(Harris, 2007).

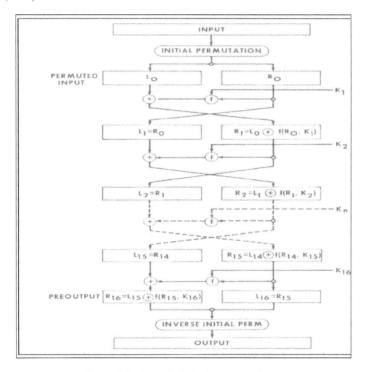

**Figure 2.4 – DES Enciphering Computation**
**Source – NIST FIPS 46-3**

These encryption standards were reviewed for the purposes of understanding encryption

technology as it has been used in the Federal Government and in the industry as a whole. While

NIST might be specific to the US Government, the commercial sector has also embraced these

standards and they have been incorporated into a multitude of commercial products. This

23

research also identified that there are multiple ways to implement the encryption standards and that in many cases, that implementation is subject to interpretation by vendors. This has an impact on long term archival of encrypted records. The fact that two vendors claim to meet, lets say TDES, does not necessarily mean that one vendor can interpret the other vendor's data or files.

DES uses a symmetric key meaning it uses the same key to encrypt and decrypt the data. These algorithms are called symmetric key algorithms. As part of this research the author also researched asymmetric encryption algorithm standards that use two different encryption keys. Asymmetric algorithms are commonly known as public key encryption. "Public key cryptography is an encryption scheme that allows private communications to take place without prior existence of a shared secret" (Tulloch, 2003). Since public key encryption does not need a shared key, like symmetric encryption does, it became a de facto standard for exchanging secret keys used by symmetric encryption algorithms. Public key algorithms in conjunction with PKI (described in chapter one), which are used today to provide legally binding electronic signatures, are the only form of encryption currently being addressed by The National Archives and Records Administration. For this purpose, the author reviewed FIPS PUB 186-2 Digital Signature Standard also known as DSS (NIST, 2000). It should be noted that this standard is currently being reviewed and a draft was published in 2006 under FIPS PUB 186-3 (NIST, 2006). The changes being proposed are mainly to update the algorithms with more recent ones.

NIST SP 800-21, "Guideline for Implementing Cryptography in the Federal Government", provides high-level guidance on how to implement encryption and includes some suggestions for key management. This guide recommends encryption keys be archived for a sufficiently long Cryptoperiod (NIST, 2005). NIST warns implementers that "Keys may be archived for a lengthy period (on the order of decades), so that they can be used to verify

signatures and decrypt ciphertext" (NIST, 2005).

Another NIST standard included in this research is NIST SP 800-57 "Recommendations

for Key Management"; which was published in 2007. This publication provides guidance and

possible alternatives/approaches to address specific research sub-question number two: Can

encryption codes be stored for long periods of time and be linked to the encrypted records? In

2001, OMB issued memorandum 11-01 "OMB Guidance to Federal Agencies on Data

Availability and Encryption" (OMB, 2001). In such guidance, OMB indicates that NIST would

issue appropriate guidance to agencies and such guidance is provided in NIST SP 800-57.

NIST SP 800-57 provides descriptions and processes that may be useful in addressing

key management. According to NIST, key management is "the activities involving the handling

of cryptographic keys and other related security parameters (e.g., IVs and passwords) during the

entire life cycle of the keys, including their generation, storage, establishment, entry and output,

and destruction" (NIST, 2007). The concept of a cryptoperiod is also introduced in this

document. Cyrptoperiod can be the timeframe a particular key is authorized for use, or, it can be

the time period the key remains in effect for a system or an application. The guidance provided

by NIST for encrypted data is that the encryption keys need to be archived, protected, and

retained until the end of the lifetime of the data. Unfortunately, this is in conflict with the generic

guidance to change these keys every 2-3 years. The reason behind this guidance is that the

confidence of the confidentiality of the data will go down as time passes. This is due to several

factors, including the fact that encryption algorithms can be broken, as DES was broken, and the

fact that computers are becoming more and more powerful while at the same time being less

expensive which allows for the possibility of brute force attacks being successful.

The document also mentions the use of a key repository called a key management archive that can be used to store encryption keys for archival purposes. Several types of additional encryption keys are mentioned in NIST SP 800-57. Of particular interest for this research paper are keys that can be used to protect keys; terms for these include symmetric key wrapping keys and key encrypting keys. These keys could be used to protect other keys. As an example, you could do a yearly encrypted back-up and then keep all the yearly keys in a file that has been encrypted with a master encryption key. If you need to retrieve a file years from now you could use the master key to decrypt the key history file and pull out the key for that year. One caveat in this scenario is that the key history file would need to be stored and maintained separate from the actual encrypted data.

As mentioned throughout this paper, encryption keys are one large piece of the puzzle but so are the software used to provide the encryption. In terms of the software, NIST provides guidance under a section entitled "Association with Usage or Application". It is pretty clear that NIST is concerned that loosing such association could lead to data loss. They suggest either associating the keys with its usage or application as they are being distributed, or have the application itself implicitly define it. To accomplish this association NIST recommends the use of identifiers and labels. The identifier links the information protected by the key and the key itself. This "identifier" information can be stored with the key in an identification label or it can be stored with the protected information. NIST provides the following examples as to the types of information that a label should include (NIST, 2007):

1. Key identifier
2. Information identifying associated keys (e.g., the association between a public and private key)
3. Identity of the key's owner or the sharing entity

4. Cryptoperiod (e.g., start date and end date)

5. Key type (e.g., signing private key, encryption key, master key)

6. Application (e.g., purchasing, email)

7. Counter – if needed

8. Domain parameters (e.g., the domain parameters used by DSA or ECDSA, or a pointer to them)

9. Status or state of the key

10. Key encrypting key identifier (e.g., key wrapping key identifier, algorithm for the key wrapping algorithm, etc.)

11. Integrity protection mechanism (e.g., key and algorithm used to provide cryptographic protection, and protection code (e.g., MAC, digital signature))

12. Other information (e.g., length of the key, protection requirements, who has access rights, additional conditions for use)

The association of keys to the information and/or the application, together with the use of identifying labels, can be part of a comprehensive solution to address sub-question number two: Can encryption codes be stored for long periods of time and be linked to the encrypted records?

In chapter one we described what a public key infrastructure (PKI) is and how it works. In essence, a PKI includes programs, data formats, protocols, processes, procedures, and public key cryptographic mechanism all working together in a comprehensive matter to provide encryption services. PKI is oriented towards public key encryption, which is what most e-mail encryption programs use. As explained in chapter one, PKI uses X.509 digital certificates. The most common standard for e-mail encryption is S/MIME, which is based on the Multipurpose Internet Mail Extension (MIME) technical specification. S/MIME uses X.509 certificates for encrypting and signing e-mail as well as e-mail attachments. The PKI is responsible for generating certificates and storing them. One key service provided by the PKI is key recovery and key/certificate archival. Since certificates are only valid for a couple of years, the PKI can keep track of certificates for historical purposes but also to be able to decrypt a file that was encrypted with an older certificate. This would be the case of encrypted e-mail or encrypted files that have been archived and place in long term storage.

## Long-term archival and preservation of digital information

For libraries, the possibility of loosing digital records or access to such digital records has been a topic of discussion for quite a while. The same applies to government agencies since on many cases they are responsible for the preservation of critical records including, but not limited to, historical records, toxic waste disposal records, medical research records, environmental data, Census data, etc.

In his article entitled "Ensuring the Longevity of Digital Information", Jeff Rothenberg (1999) cites a couple of cases in which digital records were lost. One well-known example was the loss of Census data from 1960. In that case, the data was lost because it was stored on digital tapes that became obsolete. A much older report from 1990 by the House of Representatives entitled "Taking a byte out of history: the archival preservation of federal computer records" cites at least seven other cases in which government digital record were lost.

Lehman, in his report entitled "Making the Transitory Permanent: The Intellectual Heritage in a Digitized World of Knowledge," identifies 6 characteristics and circumstances that pose the greatest danger to the long term availability of digital publications (Lehman, 1996, p.311-312):

1. Physical deterioration of digital information
2. Changes in coding formats
3. Changes in software, operating systems, and hardware
4. System-based causes

5. Economic limitations

6. Radical delocalization of processing and decentralization of databases

Physical deterioration deals mainly with the lifespan of the physical medial itself. Magnetic media like backup tapes and floppy disks have a lifetime of only a few years. After that the magnetic particles start loosing magnetism and data is lost. According to Lehman, digital media can last for up to 50 years. Digital media includes CD-ROMs and DVDs.

Changes in coding and format problems are associated with changes in programming languages, incompatibility between software versions, and changes on file formats. An example of such changes would be the change in file formats introduced by Microsoft on its latest version of Windows Office. Microsoft made a change from the Object Linking and Embedding (OLE) format to the Extensible Markup Language (XML) file format. From an encryption point of view, we use the example of changing from information that has been encrypted using DES as opposed to AES.

Changes in software have a substantial impact when a market leader starts loosing market share and may eventually run out of business. On example of that would be the change in word processing standards from WordPerfect to Microsoft Word. Operating systems also change but their changes are less frequent; probably due to the fact that it takes a while for major corporations to deploy a new version of an operating system. Examples of changes in this area include the change from Control Program for Microcomputers (CPM) to Microsoft Disk Operating System (MS-DOS) to Microsoft Windows. Changes in operating system can be linked to changes in hardware. The CPM operating system would run on 8 bit Intel 8080 microprocessors, MS-DOS runs on the 16 bit Intel 8086 microprocessor, and now the Pentium dual core 64 bit microprocessors that can run Microsoft Windows Vista.

System-based causes include such items as hypertext documents, which only exist as long as the network exists. Another type of system based would be Wikipedia, which is constantly updated/corrected by users.

Economic limitations are associated with economic value of information as time passes. For example, a TIME magazine article might provide information that is useful for weeks or months and might not be worth storing for decades.

Radical delocalization of processing and decentralization of databases is most concerned with information being stored all over the world, sometimes on a single server by the author. If the authors pull it off the server, or the server is removed permanently from the network, the information would be lost.

Of particular importance for this research paper are changes in coding formats and changes in software, operating systems, and hardware.

Literature review identified three key areas currently being researched to address the preservation of digital records: Migration, translation, and emulators. Encryption was briefly mentioned by Ross and Gow (1999) on their study titled "Digital Archeology: Rescuing Neglected and Damaged Data Resources" as an area that warranted further work. However, Ross and Gow (1999) only looked at encryption as a tool that could be used to decode bit sequences to interpret file formats not encrypted records.

"Migration is a set of organized tasks designed to achieve the periodic transfer of digital material from one hardware/software configuration to another, or from one generation of computer technology to a subsequent generation" (Task Force on Archiving of Digital Information, 1996). The literature review identified that most efforts in this area were focused on transferring digital records from one media to another. Examples include the transfer of files from magnetic tape to floppy disk to CD ROM. The main focus of these research efforts is the deterioration of digital media.

Translation is focused on writing software that can take a file in one format and translate it into a newer format. The proponents of this methodology claim that by doing this every time there is a file format change; the digital record could be retained and interpreted in the future. A variation of this approach was proposed by Lorie (2000) in his IBM Research Report entitled "Long-Term Archiving of Digital Information. He approach was to develop a standard to archive digital records with metadata that would describe the methods used to access the data. The method in this context is the behavior of the program used to access the file. The following figure illustrates the overall mechanism.

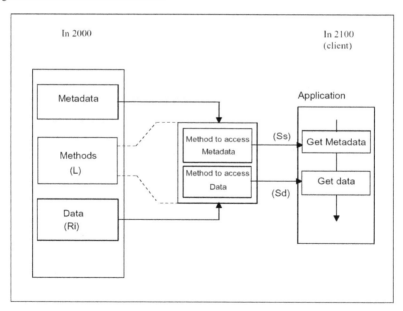

**Figure 2.5 - Overall mechanism for data archiving**
**Source – IBM Research Report – Long Term Archiving of Digital Information**

31

One key deterrent to translation is that the digital record is changed during each translation and there is a risk of loosing key pieces of information during the translation.

Emulators attempt to recreate the hardware and software necessary to run the program needed to interpret the data. Ross and Gow (1999), on their study titled "Digital Archeology: Rescuing Neglected and Damaged Data Resources," grouped emulators into three categories: Processor emulation, operating system emulation, and machine emulations.

In his report "Avoiding Technological Quicksand: Finding a Viable Technical Foundation for Digital Preservation," Dr. Rothenberg makes a clear case that digital documents are inherently software dependent, hence, the need for emulators. He states that "digital documents exist only by virtue of software that understands how to access and display them; they come into existence only by virtue of running this software" (Rothenberg, 1999). It should be noted that Lorie (2000), from IBM, disagreed with Rothenberg's approach to archiving digital records. Lorie's main contention was that if all you needed was to display/view the digital document why would you need to emulate the whole program that does much more than display it (e.g., create, edit, retouch). Lorie considered this overkill. Lorie's proposal was to create something similar to a document viewer. Granted most of the research on these topics is 5-10 years old and emulation software, like VMware, has made it rather trivial to emulate a computer system that includes hardware, processor, and operating system software.

Extensive research by the author of this paper has found no information related to the loss of encrypted records and only one source related to long term storage of electronic records that have been digitally signed (through the use of encryption technology and standards). The one source was the National Archives and Records Administration (NARA), the Federal Government agency responsible for providing guidance on record retention for all federal agencies. However,

32

NARA's focus has been on retention of records that have been digitally signed and the requirement to prove the validity of the signature over a long period of time. On March 11, 2005, NARA published the following document: Records Management Guidance for PKI Digital Signature Authenticated and Secured Transaction Records. In such guidance, NARA (2005) specifically states that "Records related to the use of PKI technology for encrypting transaction content in order to protect its privacy and confidentiality is out of scope for this guidance." The capability of being able to retrieve encrypted records from long term storage and retrieval is an important topic of concern.

The NARA guidance requires government agencies to be able to recreate the complete PKI infrastructure in order to validate the authenticity of the digital signatures. Their document does provide very detailed information on the types of data that needs to be preserved, including encryption algorithms and keys. However, NARA's approach can be quite an expensive and technically complicated proposition. The author of this paper was not able to identify any government agency that has implemented such a capability. Virtual Computing Software might make this proposition more feasible.

Virtual Computing Software

According to VMware, the leading vendor of virtual computing software, "the term virtualization broadly describes the separation of a resource or request for a service from the underlying physical delivery of that service" (Woods, 2007). In essence, virtualization software allows users to run several virtual computers on one hardware platform/device. For example, you could purchase a DELL computer running Microsoft Windows XP and load a copy of VMware to create a couple of virtual computers running Linux or Solaris. In the end, you would have 2-3 computers running on one piece of hardware.

A good understanding of virtual computing software is important in order to start the analysis of specific research sub-question three: What is the current state of Virtual Computing Machines software and can this software be used to address some of the problems associated with long term retrieval of encrypted records?

Virtual machine software is not new; it dates back to the 1960's when IBM used it to partition expensive mainframe systems into multiple virtual mainframes (Lohr, 2007). One major recent development in this technology was the introduction of VMware back in 1998. VMware brought virtual machine software to the masses by developing software that would run and take advantage of much cheaper processor platforms (e.g., Intel and AMD x86 platforms).

It could be said that a VMware virtual machine is a type of emulator; however, there are some fundamental differences. An emulator will attempt to emulate all types of hardware associated with the machine it is emulating; whether that hardware exists on the machine it is running on or not. This makes the emulators much slower in performance. In VMware, the physical hardware of the computer is considered the host machine, while the virtual machine is considered a guest. VMware virtualizes things like video adapters, network adapters, and hard disk. The host itself provides drivers that pass information between the guest and the actual hardware. Emulators can't do this. The end result is that you could stop and freeze a VMware guest, save it to a file, move it to another computer, load the VMware image, and continue at the point the machine was stopped/frozen.

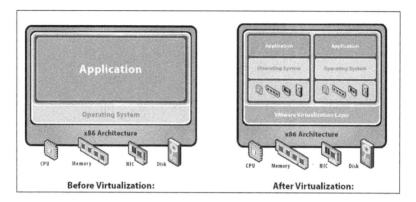

**Figure 2.6 - VMware Virtualization**
**Source – VMware Virtualization Overview Whitepaper**

Until recently virtual computing software was not robust enough for an enterprise level

deployment. Additionally, the cost per machine needed to be factored in and the products that

required activation (e.g., Microsoft Windows) would not work properly in such environments

because they were tied to a piece of hardware. These factors have changed recently. Most

vendors, including Microsoft and VMware, now offer free versions of their virtual software.

With the introduction of hardware support for virtual software, products like Microsoft Windows

can now run on any machine, whether it is a virtual machine or a physical machine.

Several benefits of virtual computing software have contributed to its popularity.

VMware mentions 4 in their Virtualization Overview whitepaper: Server consolidation, test and

development optimization, business continuity, and enterprise desktop (Virtualization Overview,

2007). The author of this paper is most interested in the enterprise desktop, whereby the image

of the operating system and the encryption software could be archived for long periods of time,

quickly retrieved, and executed to provide access to encrypted records.

According to Jack Loftus (2006), in his article "Virtual Iron adds Xen; aims for rival

VMware," research firms like IDC and Forrester Research have claimed that virtualization will

be built into every layer of IT within the next five years. Margie Semilof (2006), on her article

entitled "VM market on fire with software giveaways", goes on to mention a Gartner Inc.

prediction that "within three years roughly 40% to 50% of servers will actually be running

virtual machines." IDC, Forrester Research, and Gartner are considered to be some of the

world's top IT research firms.

IDC shows a robust virtual machine software (VMS) market growth in the past couple of

years. From 2004 to 2005 the market grew 50%, and from 2005 to 2006 the market grew by an

outstanding 69% (Rose & Humphreys, 2007). The following table shows IDC's worldwide

virtual machine software forecast for 2007-2011.

| | 2005 | 2006 | 2007 | 2008 | 2009 | 2010 | 2011 |
|---|---|---|---|---|---|---|---|
| 2007 forecast | NA | 1,045 | 1,384 | 1,882 | 2,549 | 3,101 | 3,472 |
| Growth (%) | NA | NA | 32.4 | 36.0 | 35.4 | 21.7 | 12.0 |
| 2006 forecast | 560 | 819 | 1,085 | 1,312 | 1,542 | 1,799 | NA |
| Growth (%) | NA | 46.2 | 32.4 | 20.9 | 17.5 | 16.7 | NA |

**Table 2.1 - Worldwide Virtual Machine Software Forecast for 2007-2011**
**Source – IDC Worldwide Virtual Machine Software 2007-2011 Forecast – Market**
**Analysis.**

As part of this research paper the author has also reviewed VMware Server and VMware

Player user manuals available at www.vmware.com. Web sites that provide instructions on how

to build a Windows 95 virtual image have also been researched. VMware Server can run on a

desktop and allows the user to run multiple x86-compatible operating system instances on one

single PC as virtual machines. These virtual machines are portable and can be moved from one

desktop to another as long as the other desktops also run on an x-86 hardware platform. The

36

process for doing this is to obtain a copy of a VMware server or workstation, and run it on a Windows desktop or server. Once the initial VMware software is loaded it will prompt the user for the operating system disks and start building a virtual machine of that operating system just like if it were another PC. Unfortunately, VMware Workstation is not free but can be downloaded for a 30-day evaluation period. VMware server, on the other hand, is available free of charge. There are other products that are available, some of which are becoming increasingly popular. One such product that started as freeware is XEN; but similar to VMware (which was purchased by EMC Corporation), XEN has been purchased by Citrix Corporation. One advantage of XEN is that it uses open source. One disadvantage is that it only runs on Linux operating system not on the Microsoft Windows operating system.

VMware Player, unlike VMware Workstation, is free and it allows any user to run virtual machines created with VMware Workstation or VMware Server. Users can download a free copy from VMware's website. The big difference between the products is that the VMware Player user cannot modify virtual machines created with VMware Workstation/Server. VMware Server is also available as a free download. The advantage is that the user could create an image to demonstrate a capability of a software package and then make multiple copies to send to interested parties. The interested parties could see how it works and take the virtual image for a test drive. For the purposes of this research paper, the advantage is that you could save virtual images of operating systems including the encryption software and the encryption keys, together with data backups. The player could also be saved with the backups. Many years from now when a need arises to access that encrypted data, the user can run the virtual image with VMware Player and access the encrypted data. Granted the encryption key would need to be available.

A freeware version of Pretty Good Privacy (PGP) for Windows 95 has been downloaded for further research. Manuals for PGP and the software were retrieved from www.pgpi.org. PGP was a very popular e-mail encryption package in the mid to late 1990s. PGP uses its own digital certificates as opposed to PKI certificates. However, PGP certificates serve the same purpose. With PGP, instead of relying on a Certificate Authority like VeriSign to trust other users, you rely on a circle of trust, or shall we say, a circle of friends. With PGP, users generate their own encryption keys and then share their public key with friends. If someone you do not know wants to communicate with you, you can ask a mutual friend to vouch for or "introduce" the unknown user. Keys from your circle of friends are kept in a file called a key ring.

The way PGP works is by encrypting data with a one-time session key. The session key is generated using random numbers triggered by the movement of your mouse. The session key is then encrypted with the recipient's public key. Then the message and the encrypted session key are sent via e-mail to the recipient. The recipient uses their private key to decrypt the session key, which, in turn, is used to decrypt the message with the same encryption algorithm used by the sender. PGP also uses compression to speed the encryption process and to speed up transmission.

Due to the recent developments in the virtual computing software market, the possibility of using virtual computing software to save an image of a computer, including its operating systems and encryption software, has become quite feasible. This by itself will not solve all the problems dealing with long term archival of encrypted records, but it can be part of a process or part of a comprehensive solution. If you look at NARA's (2005) expensive and slightly unrealistic proposition to save a complete copy/instantiation of the PKI infrastructure in order to validate the electronic signature on digital records, it now becomes a possibility.

CHAPTER 3: What happens when organizations are unable to retrieve records from long-term storage?

The Office of Management and Budget defines personally identifiable information (PII) as "any information about an individual maintained by an agency, including, but not limited to, education, financial transactions, medical history, and criminal or employment history and information which can be used to distinguish or trace an individual's identity, such as their name, social security number, date and place of birth, mother's maiden name, biometric records, etc., including any other personal information which is linked or linkable to an individual" (OMB, 2006). PII data has received a lot of attention in recent years because organized crime is using such data to perform identity theft. Once an identity has been stolen, criminals use that information for financial gain. One way criminals do this is by applying for credit cards under the stolen identity, running the credit card to its limit and not paying it. Another technique used by criminals is to use PII data to gain access to bank accounts and transfer funds out of the victims account.

Loss or compromise of PII data has financial implications for both the organization that lost the data and for the individual. If the data is lost but not used to commit identity theft it still has some considerable financial implications for the organization. Take the example of the data breach in 2006 at the Department of Veteran's Affairs where PII data for 17.5 million veterans and military personnel was stolen. In this case the Department offered to pay credit monitoring for about $75 a year. This incident could have cost the agency up to 1.5 billion dollars a year. On the other hand, if the data were used to commit identity theft, it would have serious consequences for individuals in terms of loosing credit and spending time and resources repairing their credit. The number of PII data breaches is quite startling. As of May 13, 2007, the Privacy Rights Clearing House had reported several incidents where a total of 226,885,128 records containing sensitive personal information had been exposed. The Clearing House has been tracking data breaches in the U.S. since January 2005 (Privacy Rights Clearing House, 2008). The Clearing House updates and publishes this data everyday on their web site at www.privacyrights.org.

According to the 2007 Javelin Strategy & Research Survey on Identity Fraud conducted for the Federal Trade Commission, the number of reported instances of identity theft has been coming down in the past few years. However, the statistics remain quite high. The survey findings include:

- The number of US adult victims of identity fraud decreased from 10.1 million in 2003 and 9.3 million in 2005 to 8.4 million in 2007.
- Total one-year fraud amount decreased from $55.7 billion in 2006 to $49.3 billion in 2007.
- The mean fraud amount per fraud victim decreased from $6,278 in 2006 to $5,720 in 2007.
- The mean resolution time was at a high of 40 hours per victim in 2006 and was reduced in 2007 to 25 hours per victim. The median resolution time has remained the same for each Survey year at 5 hours per victim

The alarming statistics of data breaches and identity theft cases have prompted organizations to use encryption as the tool of choice for protecting PII data. In the Federal Government, OMB has mandated such encryption for laptops that may contain PII data. OMB memorandum M-06-16 also recommends encryption for PII being transported and/or stored offsite. This includes data that is being stored for long-term archival purposes. What happens when the encryption key or the encryption software used to encrypt these records is changed? If the encryption keys are not properly managed, or the encryption software is not backed up, it can render the data useless. In other words, the criminals cannot read it but neither can the agency.

In an interview with M.R., senior engineer with the Mitre Corporation, he provided another example of what could be the impact of lost keys or incompatible encryption keys. His example was related to the implementation of the advanced access content system (AACS) for copyright protection of movie DVDs and music CDs. In this example, Mr. R. points to the futile attempts by the Motion Picture Association of America to control encryption keys used by DVD/CD player manufacturers as well as audio/video software developers. It seems like every time the Motion Picture Association changes the key, hackers on the Internet quickly crack the code and publish the new key. At one point the Association tried to send cease and desist letters to website administrators asking them to remove the keys from their sites. Such tactic backfired and hackers started posting the keys on all kinds of sites. This made enforcement pretty futile. Another side effect of using the AACS type of encryption and key management that is built into hardware, also mentioned by Mr. R. during the interview, is that when the published key were revoked and changed, CD and DVD players could no longer play newer DVDs or CDs. This would require users to purchase new players. The reader of this paper can probably see the analogy here of not being able to read archival data due to incorrect or invalid encryption keys.

The inability to access encrypted records also has implications for law enforcement. In a well-known case in 2006 in the United Kingdom, a gang of ID thieves were arrested and prosecuted. However, the extent of their crimes will probably never be known because the records on their computer were all encrypted. In this case, the police were not able to decrypt the files. According to an article published in ZDNet-UK "it would have taken 400 computers twelve years to crack the code" (CNET Networks, 2006). The thieves were successfully

prosecuted due to other evidence.

The implications of not being able to access electronic records are best explained using a

couple of scenarios.


Scenario One: Loss of taxpayer data

The Internal Revenue Service (IRS) processes millions of tax returns a year and collects

trillions of dollars a year in tax revenue. With so many tax returns and so much money it can be

assumed that the IRS is a prime target for PII data and that such data could be used to commit tax

fraud. In this hypothetical example, the criminal might want to submit a fraudulent tax return for

an older person that has died but whose death has not been reported. That person was receiving

social security checks and paying taxes on such income. The criminal has been perpetrating this

crime for years and changing his address periodically. Let's say that criminals have figured out

that this crime can succeed if the criminals change their address every year because it takes the

Social Security Administration and the IRS a couple of years to synchronize their databases.

At the IRS, the Inspector General (IG) is responsible for investigating and prosecuting tax

fraud. Let's say the IRS keeps tax payer data on-line for 3 years and stores tax payer data offsite

every year and that data is encrypted. Let's say the IG has detected this tax fraud a couple of

times this past year. The IG would like to find out if there is any pattern to this type of fraud.

The one common pattern the investigator finds is that the criminals change their address every

year before April 15. To see if this pattern can be useful in detecting fraud, let's assume the

investigator searches the on-line taxpayers records and identifies 100 tax returns that fit this

pattern. Upon further research, the investigator identifies 10 fraudulent tax returns out of the

100. Very pleased with his 10% hit rate, the investigators boss asks that he run it on tax returns going back 10 years. To do this, the investigator will need to pull records from archival storage. When he tries to load the data from the encrypted tape backups, the software is unable to read the records because they are encrypted or because the software to read the records is not available. The investigator calls the IT department for help and they tell him that they only back up data after three years but not the programs. Let's say the encryption software vendor has copies of the program and in the spirit of good citizenship they provide the IRS with a free copy. As the IT department is loading the software, the program requests an encryption key. The IT department calls the investigator for the key but the investigator explains that he has nothing to do with encryption software for back-up tapes, that that is the responsibility of the IT department. The IT department scrambles but finds out no one keeps copies of encryption keys.

In this scenario, the implications are loss of revenue as well as not being able to prosecute people that have committed this type of tax fraud in the past. However, the implications are far greater because this would apply to any other type of tax fraud pattern that extends multiple years. Further complicating the matter is that even if current criminals are caught, the IRS would only be able to go back 3 years and prosecute for that amount. Like many other crimes, sentencing guidelines are usually tied to the dollar amounts of the crime. The higher the dollar amount the longer the sentence.

Scenario Two: Loss of Corporate data needed for a Security and Exchange Commission (SEC) investigation.

In this example we will use an energy company, like Enron, in which several executives as well as the external auditing firm were accused of fraud. In Enron's case, the executives were

43

manipulating the financial statements to make it look like the company was doing well. One technique they were using was the creation of fictitious corporations. Let's say the president and the chief financial officer (CFO) exchanged quite a bit of e-mails related to the legality of the questionable bookkeeping practices being used by the corporation. Let's also say the financial records of these fictitious corporations were being stored in encrypted form and the encryption key was being changed every year. Encryption keys were kept on floppy disks that were not very well guarded, maybe intentionally.

Let's say the SEC moved in and took over the electronic records and made copies of them and took them offsite for further analysis. During such analysis they discovered e-mails and tape backups have been encrypted. When questioned by the investigators, the president and CFO have no clue and say that that is the IT department's responsibility. The technician that was changing keys every year left the corporation over a year ago when the corporation was starting to have financial troubles. When questioned by the investigators he says the diskettes with the keys were in his desk. However, his desk has been cleaned/emptied since he left and now a new technician has it. In summary, the data contained in encrypted e-mails and tape backups are no longer accessible.

In this scenario, the impact to the investigators and prosecutors is that their case is much weaker, with less evidence. Additionally, the money trail as to where the fictitious companies where the funds were being transferred will probably be lost.

This scenario can be expanded to many other situations. Let's say you have another Watergate incident where the White House and the President were involved in some type of illegal activity. Encryption can be used as a way to hide possible evidence.

44

One factor complicating e-mail encryption is the availability of free e-mail encryption software like Pretty Good Privacy. Many corporations have avoided implementing a public key infrastructure (PKI) due to the costs and vendor-survival uncertainty. A PKI would manage encryption keys and protect the corporation against a disgruntled employee or a dishonest employee using encryption to hide information. Since the PKI maintains copies of every employee's keys for years, the corporation would be able to decrypt the data. By not investing in a PKI many users have gone out and installed PGP to encrypt e-mails. Unfortunately, PGP encryption keys are maintained by the user not the corporation.

During an interview with Ms. C. L., forensic fraud investigator for Siemens USA, she elaborated on the impact of electronic records not being available for an internal investigation and indicated it has more to do with the level of confidence and the comprehensiveness of an internal case. Ms. L. did provide the author of this paper with a pointer to a well know case in which an old e-mail became the pivotal piece of key evidence and it just happens to be related to Enron.

In her article entitled "Enron's jury's told the proof is in the e-mail", Mary Flood (2004), a reporter with the Houston Chronicle, explains how an e-mail would prove former Enron executives conspired with Merrill Lynch bankers in order to illegally boost Enron's profits to meet Wall Street expectations. This case is related to Enron's purchase of several energy producing barges from Nigeria. The case involved a transaction between Enron and Merrill Lynch whereby Enron asked the banker to buy the Barges from Enron so it could book the sale as revenue and collect bonuses for its executives. After the sale and after earnings reports came out, Enron would buy the barges back from Merrill Lynch. The proof that Merrill Lynch knew about this illegal transaction was contingent on an e-mail between an Enron executive and

Merrill Lynch bankers. In the end, Merrill Lynch settled with the SEC without admitting any

guilt. Ironically, additional e-mails that would have implicated Merrill Lynch even more were

lost when the World Trade Center was attacked and destroyed by terrorists.


Scenario Three: Loss of research data

Let's use the example of a pharmaceutical company that has been working on a cancer

drug. Pharmaceutical companies are extremely protective of their research data in order to keep

their competitive edge. Let's say the company maintains on-line data for five years at which

time it backs up the data and stores it off-site. To protect research data that is stored off-site the

company encrypts the data. Ten years ago they worked on a promising drug but the side effects

were too dangerous so it did not go to market. Millions of dollars were invested on such

research. Just recently the company has found a way to eliminate the majority of the side effects

with another drug. When they try to pull the research data from tapes dated back ten years ago

they find out they have lost the encryption key.

In this scenario, the loss is not only in terms of millions of research dollars but also in

terms of delaying a drug that has the potential of saving tens of thousands of individuals.

In an interview with S. B., Lead Information Security Engineer with the Mitre

Corporation, she explained the requirements for encryption and long term archival of records in

the pharmaceutical industry. Prior to Mitre, Ms. B. spent many years working in the

pharmaceutical industry, including a stint with Warner-Lambert (a Fortune 100 global

pharmaceutical/consumer products company which was acquired by Pfizer, Inc.). According to

Ms. B., this industry has several regulatory requirements to store data for many years. She

explained that for every drug that goes to market, pharmaceutical companies are required to keep three types of information: 1. Information from the results of independent clinical trails for the drug. 2. Information provided to the FDA to get the drug approved. 3. Any information on unanticipated adverse events related to people taking the drug. The first two types of information are public information but the third one is corporate private information. One example of confidential data she provided was related to diabetes drugs whereby the clinical trails did not include minorities. After the drug was released, Blacks and Hispanics started to have adverse events.

When asked during the interview about retention and encryption requirements for the pharmaceutical companies, Ms. B. indicated this industry is regulated by the Code of Federal Regulations (CFR) 21. According to her, it mandates encryption and storage of drug related data for seven years. However, she did warn the author that once an investigation is started or there is a lawsuit, the data can be kept and stored for many more years. Ms. B. also indicated that it was not just backing up data in encrypted form but also the software needed to read that data.

In terms of processes and techniques used to encrypt data, Ms. B. indicated that the companies she worked for had a PKI and that once a year during disaster recovery testing, her company would test the encryption software, key recovery, and hardware needed to read the tapes. She also indicated her company used key escrow.

Interviews with industry experts

In May 2008, interviews were conducted with industry experts on electronic fraud and internal information systems audits.

C. L. is the manager of the Computer Forensics and Electronic Evidence Division for Siemens USA. Prior to working for Siemens, Ms. L. worked as a crime investigator for law enforcement. Her current job involves fraud investigations, internal audits, and whistle blowers. Her office gets involved once a compliance officer determines probable cause.

During the interview, Ms. L. addressed the implications of not being able to access encrypted e-mail. She indicated that in many cases, the reason why old e-mails are not accessible is due to the record retentions policies of organizations. If an organization has a retention policy of only 3 months that is all that is available to a forensics investigator like her. She cites a couple of reasons for this. One is the fact that corporations need to strike a balance between keeping too much and keeping too little. Keeping too much could provide more evidence against the corporation in the case they are sued. On the other hand, too little information can hinder an internal investigation. According to her, the requirement to keep backups of corporate data for long periods of time are mostly driven by external regulatory requirements, but e-mail records are not included under those regulations. She did clarify that once an investigation is launched, internally or externally, then, all records, including e-mail, can be kept for many years.

S. B.-H. is a Lead Information Security Engineer with the Mitre Corporation, a federally funded research and development center. Prior to joining Mitre, S. worked on various projects for major pharmaceutical and security companies. As a consultant for a Fortune 500 pharmaceutical company in New Jersey, she served as the Head of Security for the in-house Privacy Program in the Research Division.

When asked what would be the consequences of not being able to read data from archival records, Ms. B. indicated, "That is just not an option." Ms. B. cited the example of a diabetes drug called "Rezulin" that was pulled off the market. The drug company had very few cases of unanticipated adverse events in their confidential records. Then an L.A. reporter started to report on problems with Rezulin and all of the sudden more than 150 cases were reported including a

48

couple of deaths. According to Ms. B., when this happens, the potential for lawsuits increases

dramatically. If the drug company is not able to build a strong case in court using its own data

then the losses would be in the millions of dollars. She re-emphasized, "It's just not an option."

CHAPTER 4: Encryption keys backup and recovery

Chapter three provides some convincing evidence stating that valuable sensitive data should be protected and one method that will be required will be encryption. However, encryption, if not properly managed, can cause data to be unreadable. Chapter three also provides some examples on what would be the impact to organizations that are unable to retrieve valuable information from long term archival storage. Being that more and more organizations today will be encrypting their data, this chapter will explore the guidance available for handling encryption and encrypted data. This chapter will also identify some examples on how some organizations and some vendors are providing tools to manage encryption and encryption keys while also providing for key management and key recovery.

S. B. (2001), in his book Writing Information Security Policies, does not recommend encrypting archive and backup data. His main concern has to do with the complexity key management and key recovery for each copy of the media. B. recommends good physical security controls as a compensating control. B.'s advice was probably adequate in 2001, when his book was published, but as expressed in chapter three, the threat against sensitive data has substantially increased. With organized crime now benefiting financially from stealing PII data, it should come as no surprise that many organizations are now encrypting their tape backups. A Google search for "OMB – data – encryption backups" will return quite a number of results for government agencies that are trying to comply with OMB memorandum M-07-16 "Safeguarding Against and Responding to the Breach of Personally Identifiable Information" (OMB, 2007). The memorandum requires the safeguarding of any PII data that leaves the organization's premises and many are opting for encrypting tape backups, which are often stored at offsite locations operated by private firms like Iron Mountain. A similar search on Google but replacing OMB for Sarbanes-Oxley (data security regulations that apply to the private sector) will also return a substantial number of results.

In an interview with S. B., the author of this paper was able to obtain an updated recommendation since Mr. B.'s book was published so many years ago. After some discussion of more current developments, B. still recommends not encrypting archival records due to the risks associated once you disconnect the data from the system. In terms of the recent movements to encrypt archival and back up data by many organizations, B. believes these decisions are being made by executives with a business strategic point of view but that these executives lack the technical understanding and implications of such decisions. For organizations that decide to encrypt archival data, B. recommends a PKI with appropriate key recovery policies and mechanisms.

B. has seen other approaches that can work in the short term and some that might work but are very risky. One example he provided was the case of a federal agency that uses SMIME for e-mail encryption in conjunction with Microsoft Exchange and Microsoft Active Directory products. In this example, the agency issues e-mail encryption X.509 certificates that are valid for three years. Together, the two Microsoft products can retain a copy of the current certificate and a copy of the prior certificate. In essence, this provides recoverability of encrypted e-mails for up to seven years. The other example Mr. B. provided was the example of a computer backup product that would append a file that contained the encryption keys at the end of the tape. Mr. B.'s main concern is that in such a scenario, if the tape was stolen, the thief would have access to the encryption keys.

In his book, Applied Cryptography, Bruce Schneier (1996) provides the example of a company where employees are allowed to encrypt data and the key is memorized by the employee. In his example, Mr. Schneier asks the question of what would happen if the employee gets run over by a truck. He goes on to say that all the files would be gone forever. Schneier goes on to propose a key escrow solution whereby employees would write down their keys in a piece of paper, placed them in a sealed envelop, and provide the envelop to a security officer to be stored inside a safe. A problem with this scenario is that you would have to now trust the security officer not to misuse someone's key. To address this type of problem, Mr. Schneier proposes the use of a secret-sharing protocol. With such a protocol, the user can break up the key into pieces and provide a piece of the key to different persons within the organization. To simplify this process, Mr. Schneier goes on to propose that the user encrypt each piece of the key with the other person's public key. This way the other persons would only be involved in key recovery when the user keys are lost or unavailable.

Webster's Dictionary defines escrow as "something that is delivered to a third person to be given to a grantee only upon the fulfillment of a condition" (Webtser's, 2001). In terms of key escrow, we are referring to the key as the "something." Key escrow has been controversial ever since the publication of NIST FIPS 185 Escrowed Encryption Standard (NIST, 1994). The main purpose of the standard is to provide some type of backdoor into encryption being used for telecommunications, in order for law enforcement agencies to be able to decrypt telecommunications. The standard mandated the use of the Clipper encryption chip with the Skipjack encryption algorithm developed by the National Security Agency. The politics and controversy surrounding the Clipper chip are beyond the scope of this research paper, however, the techniques and processes described in the standard should not be discounted, as they can prove useful in terms of tying keys to specific encrypted information and providing for key

recovery. For example, FIPS 185 requires the use of a Law Enforcement Access Field (LEAF).

This field in conjunction with the unique ID provided by the Clipper chip can tie a piece of

information to a particular organization and be used in conjunction with the keying material

maintained by the escrow agent to decipher the encryption keys. For the purposes of this research

paper, such an approach could be used internally whereby the organization is the escrow agent

for all users, and management controls the equivalent of a LEAF.

In an interview with M. R., senior engineer at the Mitre Corporation and the lead

engineer on the first funded High Assurance Internet Protocol Encryptor (HAIPE), he pointed the

author towards more recent key recovery encryption standard's work like the NIST document

entitled "Requirements for Key Recovery Products" (NIST, 1996). A review of that document

indicates that back in 1998, the Technical Advisory Committee to Develop a Federal Information

Processing Standard for the Federal Key Management Infrastructure was recommending the

establishment of a FIPS for key recovery products. A search of the NIST at

http://csrc.nist.gov/publications/PubsFIPS.html for a key recovery FIPS returned zero findings,

therefore, the author assumes the standard was never published. Even though the standard was

not approved, the NIST document provides some very useful guidance that can be applied to key

management and key recovery. Instead of specifying specific encryption chips or algorithms, the

document defines an abstract model for a Key Recovery System (KRS).

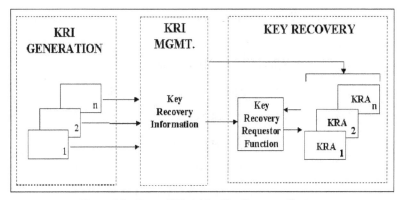

**Figure 4.1 - General Model for Key Recovery Systems**
**Source NIST- Requirements for Key Recovery Product**

In the document, NIST introduces the term of a "target key" which can be the data encryption key (DEK) used to decrypt data or it can be a key that can be used to decrypt the encrypted DEK. The KRI mentioned in Figure 4.1 refers to key recovery information needed to recover the key. The KRI can be managed by one entity or several entities called key recovery agents (KRA). The document also introduces the concept of key encapsulation technique, which is used to associate KRI with encrypted data. One fundamental difference between this document and FIPS 185 is that it recognizes the need to recover keys not only by law enforcement but organizations in the event keys are lost, or needed by the organization for its own internal monitoring purposes.

During the interview with M. R., he mentioned a couple of examples where key management or good intentions for key recovery had failed. On example was the initial of encryption for the popular file-compression software package WinZip. According to Mr. R., WinZip used to append the encryption key to the first few bytes of the encrypted zip file. As you can imagine, the file was encrypted but anyone could take the file apart and retrieve the key. The other example he provided was the example of encryption in CDs and DVDs mentioned in chapter 3.

In terms of key management, Mr. R. expressed concerns that organizations might be implementing it haphazardly and that there is even inconsistent implementations of encryption on security products. He concurs with the author of this paper that each vendor can implement the standard in many ways. Basic things like using a different initialization vectors can render two products incompatible. He mentioned the HAIPE standard and clarified that, more than an encryption standard, it is an interoperability standard to avoid interoperability issues like the ones mentioned in this paper. According to Mr. R., one of the reasons encryption is being implemented haphazardly is because "encryption is the bastard child in most CIO organizations." CIOs are concerned with keeping the IT infrastructure running and not encryption.

To learn more about how backup encryption is being implemented in large organizations, the author interviewed G. J., Chief of Tier 2 operations for IRS enterprise computing centers. The IRS used to send over 8,000 magnetic tapes that contained taxpayer information to states, backup sites, and to other government agencies like the Social Security Administration. To tackle this problem Mr. J. has implemented a three-prong approach. First, he eliminated most of the magnetic tapes by implementing secure encrypted on-line data transfers between the IRS and outside agencies. Second, he implemented encryption for backup tapes either via software encryption or hardware encryption. Third, he configured remote tape vaulting for remote sites; this way data is no longer stored at those sites and it is written to a server that resides at the computing center. Once at the computing center, it is backed up using encrypted backup technologies.

In terms of how the tape encrypting products manage keys and how his agency prepares for key recovery in the event of a disaster, Mr. J. mentioned two approaches. One is the use of a highly secure database that provides key management capabilities. This database keeps track of each tape and ties the volume/serial number to the encryption key used to encrypt it. Another prevention technique is to use different encryption keys at each computing center and send copies of the keys to each computing center.

Another NIST standard included in this research is NIST SP 800-57 "Recommendations for Key Management" (NIST, 2007). NIST SP 800-57 provides descriptions and processes that may be useful in addressing key management. The document also mentions the use of a key repository called a key management archive that can be used to store encryption keys for archival purposes. Several types of additional encryption keys are mentioned in NIST SP 800-57 including keys that can be used to protect archival keys by encrypting them.

It is pretty clear that NIST is concerned about loosing association between the application used to encrypt the data and the keys because it could lead to data loss. They suggest either associating the keys with its usage or application as they are being distributed, or, have the application itself implicitly define it.

Interview with encryption implementers and SMEs

In May 2008, interviews were conducted with implementers and subject matter experts (SME) in the area of encryption.

M. R. is a Lead Information Security Engineer with the MITRE Corporation, a federally funded research and development center. Mr. R. has 15 years experience in information security and he was the lead engineer for the first funded HAIPE project. During the interview, Mr. R.

emphasized the increased use of encryption across the military and the intelligence communities due to the fact that systems are becoming more and more mobile. Examples of mobile computing not only include laptops but smaller devices like personal digital assistants (PDA) and PocketPCs.

According to Mr. R., encryption and encryption keys comes down to whom you trust. He cites the example of electronic voting machines that use encryption "but how do you trust that the person voting is actually who they say they are." In terms of encryption keys "If you trust an employee with the encryption keys and they leave what happens then?" His preferred approach to key management would be the use of split-key-profiles whereby a pool of people have parts of the key. His example was 5 people holding parts of the key but you only need 3 of the five people to recreate the key.

G. J. is Chief of Tier 2 operations for IRS enterprise computing centers. Mr. J. manages all midlevel tax, administrative, electronic filings, compliance, and delinquent tax collection systems in the IRS. He has 31 years of experience in IT, 25 of those with the IRS. When asked about the impact of missing encryption keys during a disaster recovery scenario he indicated you would be pretty much "out of commission."

Mr. J. also expressed concerns in terms of being able to recover archival records that have been created with old and obsolete hardware. He cited the example of old nine-track tape drives used by mainframes and the fact that manufacturers of such drives are very few, if any, still remain.

S. B. is Principal Information Systems Engineer for the Mitre Corporation and the author of the book entitled Writing Information Security Policy. Mr. B. has over 25 years of IT experience, and has been with Mitre for the past seven years mostly supporting the IRS. One interesting piece of information provided by Mr. B. during the interview was that in the 1990s there was an encryption compatibility issue associated with the CPU running on personal computers. According to him, the earlier x86 processors would address memory word-by-word or byte-by-byte while newer processors do it bit-by-bit. This created some problems when trying to decrypt data that had been encrypted with the older processor.

According to Mr. B., the government works in a risk-adverse environment, hence, the rush to encrypt everything as a way to avoid a scenario like the one experienced by the VA when a laptop containing data on millions of veterans was stolen. Mr. B. advocates a more risk management process "how can I mitigate the risk to an acceptable level over the long run."

CHAPTER 5: The Current State of Virtual Computing Machines Software


Virtual computing software is software that is used to emulate the hardware of an actual

computer. By doing this in software, VM software allows for multiple computers to run on one

physical computer. These VMs can reside on a desktop or they can be retrieved from a server

and loaded onto the desktop. In other words, VMs are highly portable and not hardware

dependent. According to J. P., senior information security engineer at the Mitre Corporation,

there are three VM software manufacturers worth watching. VMware is by far the most

advanced one because it was the original developer of VM software for the Intel x86 market and

has aggressively protected its market by maintaining the software and continuously improving on

it. According to Mr. P., XEN, a VM software developed at Cambridge University, has wide

acceptance due to the fact that it came out as open source and it was freely available until

recently when Citrix Corporation bought the rights to the source code. Free older versions are

still available but newer versions will cost you. The third vendor Mr. P. recommends watching is

Microsoft. According to him, Microsoft is a latecomer into the VM market but due to its size

and market domination in the O.S. world and its renewed interest in VM software it will

eventually become a major player. Mr. P. sites Microsoft's 2006 acquisition of Softricity Inc., a

leading provider of application virtualization, as an indicator of Microsoft's intentions.

The interview with Mr. P. also provided some insights into the different types of VM

software implementations out there. For example there are some fundamental differences

between the VMware free server (used to be called GSX server) software and the commercial

version called VMware ESX server. The free version runs in full software emulation and has to

emulate all the hardware, which makes it much slower. The commercial version uses the hypervisor, which provides a layer between the physical hardware and guest operating system. He goes on to explain that XEN also runs a hypervisor model. Running a hypervisor requires modifications to the physical hardware drivers, which is why XEN would only run on Linux. Source code for Linux hardware drivers is available as open source and can be modified. Source code for Microsoft Windows is proprietary. When CPU (Intel & AMD) vendors started to provide virtualization capabilities than can run the hypervisor itself, the need to modify device drivers has gone away.

In an interview with B. B., senior computer specialist at the Internal Revenue Service (IRS), he indicated that he was of the opinion that VMware would continue to dominate the VM software market and that Microsoft had yet to deliver on their promises for an enterprise ready product. Mr. B., responsible for server consolidation and virtualization at the IRS, can foresee the IRS virtualizing a large majority of its 6,000 plus servers. The strategy he is following is to convert physical servers into virtual servers as they come up for a hardware refresh every four years. One of the advantages he cites is the capability of quickly moving legacy applications that need to run on older operating systems (e.g., Windows 2000 servers), from old hardware into newer more efficient and shared hardware. Many of these legacy applications were developed to run on a dedicated server that is, for the most part, underutilized. Virtualization also gives him the capability of moving these server-dependent applications from a campus location into a datacenter with practically no impact on the user.

Mr. B. stated that hardware support is one of the reasons why he believes VM software will eventually become a commodity and be freely available. The VM software market will transition into the management software necessary to manage virtual machines across the enterprise. J. P. concurs with Mr. B.'s opinion about VM software eventually becoming ubiquitous and free. He cites the current joint work by all the key vendors on a virtual machine format called OVF for Open Virtualization Format. This standard will allow users to move VMs from computer to computer without depending on the VM software product used to create the VM.

When asked about a good example of when VM software would be useful to recreate a retired O.S., Mr. B. provided the example of the transition from Windows NT to Windows 2000 server. He explained how certain applications were written to depend on Windows NT user profiles. The example he mentioned was an application that used an NT based fax server. These applications were transitioned into newer operating systems, but eliminating the dependency on the NT profile took quite a while. Therefore, every once in a while Mr. B. recalls having to restore a Windows NT domain to create a user profile. This would have been quite a chore, but since his organization had saved a VM image prior to retiring NT, the restoration was quick and painless.

Interview with VM implementers and researchers

In May 2008, interviews were conducted with implementers and researchers in the area of Virtual Machine Software.

B. B. is the Chief of the Server Standards and Configuration Branch of the IRS Enterprise Operations Division. He has been working for the IRS for 21 years and his responsibilities included Windows platforms, O.S. standards for all tiers, virtualization, and server consolidation. As part of his server consolidation project, Mr. B. is using VMware to consolidate servers and reduce the number of physical serves. The initial phase of his project includes the virtualization

61

of 450 servers and workstations into 47 blade servers. He is using server blades with 4 CPU and the average compression ratio, in his opinion, is 8 to 1.

Among the main benefits of VM software he cites, server consolidation, disaster recovery, and support for legacy applications. In terms of disaster recovery, Mr. B. states that "VM software gives you the capability of providing a high availability environment without the cost of high availability hardware." He provides the example of a server that might be indicating a defective hard drive whereby the server management software would move the VM server image automatically into another physical server, and then place the unhealthy server into maintenance mode.

Mr. B. foresees consolidating all servers that currently reside in over 100 locations and bringing them into their three data centers. He does mention the savings in terms of administrative, maintenance, and probable energy costs but cautions that software vendors use much higher dollar-savings figures based on the elimination of physical buildings. He indicates that in the Federal Government it is highly unlikely that the buildings that had computer rooms will go away.

The second interview in this area was with J. P., senior information security scientist at the Mitre Corporation. Mitre is a federally funded research and development center. Mr. P. has been with Mitre for five years and he came in as a recent graduate from Cornell University, where he got a master's degree in electrical computer engineering. Mr. P., who works in information security and operations, recently completed a one-year research project on virtual machine software. The research included a product survey of current VM software products. Mr. P. concluded from his research that the VM software market is fairly mature and dominated by VMware. He also concludes that several vendors are positioning themselves to play a bigger role. He gives examples of VMware being purchased by EMC, XEN being purchased by Citrix, and Microsoft's recent acquisition of Softricity. As for other vendors, he states, "Don't write IBM off quite yet, they have quite a bit of in-house expertise on virtual machines and they are doing some interesting work in their labs in terms of enforcing security policies at the hypervisor level."

Two areas of research where VMware is being used, that Mr. P. has been working on, are honeynets & trusted computing and the trusted computing initiative (TCI).

According to the Honeynet Project web site, "A honeynet is a type of honeypot. Specifically, it is a high-interaction honeypot designed to capture extensive information on threats. High-interaction means a honeynet provides real systems, applications, and services for attackers to interact with" (Honeynet Project, 2006). Mr. P. has been working with a project that uses VM software to create a VM that then goes out on the Internet and purposely tries to get infected with malware (e.g., spyware, viruses, etc.). After a couple of days, the VM is saved to a file and brought inside a lab for analysis. The infected VM is replaced with a new VM and this new VM is released again on the Internet. This allows researchers to analyze the latest malware threats in a safe environment by looking at the VM in a sandbox.

Trusted computing involves computers that can be trusted for the processing of classified data. In the past, users that were processing information at the different classification levels (e.g., Secret vs. Top Secret) would need separate physical computers. VM software, and hardware that support VMs, can be used to create two VMs on the same physical box. One VM would be approved to process Secret data, while the other VM could be approved to process Top Secret data.

When asked about the benefits of VM software as it relates to legacy systems, Mr. P. believes one of the biggest benefits will be the emulation of physical devices that might not be available. He gave the example of being able to boot from an MS-DOS diskette in order to install Windows 95. In the case of VMware, you could emulate a virtual floppy disk drive as well as a virtual floppy diskette with boot sectors. The VM would think it is accessing a physical device and media.

Virtual Machine Proof-of-Concept

The researcher was able to set up the following test scenario to demonstrate that creating a virtual machine in software and then saving it as a back up with its encryption keys would be one way of addressing long term archival of encrypted files. The following steps were taken:

1- Set up a Windows 95 VMware instantiation in an older computer
2- Load an old version of Pretty Good Privacy (PGP) encryption software
3- Load an older version of Microsoft Word
3- Encrypt a couple of files with PGP and Microsoft Word
4- Save the Image
5- Reload the image on a new PC running Windows Vista
6- Run PGP and Decrypt the files

The purpose of this exercise is to demonstrate that an environment that is 14+ years old can be easily recreated today. Most government regulations require 5-10 years for availability of the information.

The researcher will also attempt to read the files with the latest version of PGP and Microsoft Word to determine if there are any problems decrypting the files. The purpose of this second step is to determine more or less how far vendors maintain backward compatibility.

J. P. provided some VM terminology that would be useful in describing the proof-of-concept environment:

Virtual Machine (VM) – General term for all components of virtualized environment (Guest OSes, virtual HW, hypervisor, etc.)

Guest O.S. – Operating system running within a virtualized environment Often referred to as "guests," for short.

Host O.S. – The OS on which the VM runs in native and OS-level virtualization

Virtual Machine Monitor (VMM) – Generic term for the management layer in a virtual machine

Hypervisor – Management layer used by some forms of virtualization that sits between hardware and guests - Similar in concept to a microkernel

The researcher selected the VMware-Server version 1.05, the freeware version of VMware. The fact that this fully functional version of VMware is free, validates the comments made by Mr. B. and Mr. P. during the interviews who mentioned that the VM software will eventually be provided free of charge. VMware basic requirements for Microsoft Windows include a standard x86 server with a 32 bit CPU with enough memory and hard disk storage to run the host O.S. and the VM. The VMware documentation indicates only Windows 2000 server and Windows 2003 Server are supported. The platform selected for the proof-of-concept was a 1999 computer with an AMD processor running Windows XP Professional, 512 megabytes of RAM, and 120 Gigabytes of Hard disk storage. While XP professional is not supported by VMware, the author wanted to try it because XP professional includes several server extensions. The VMware server software installed with no problems.

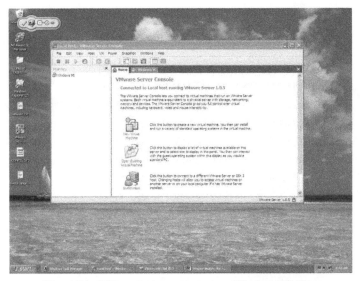

**Figure 5.1 - VMware server running on a Windows XP Host**

The next step was to build a Windows 95 virtual machine. The part of the proof-of-concept proved to be the most challenging, not because of technical problems but because the software was hard to find.

The author was able to find a Windows 95 CD-ROM, but in order to load it into the VM, the virtual hard disk had to be partitioned and formatted using MS-DOS; an even older operating system. To partition and format the hard disk, the system would need to boot from a floppy disk. Additionally, the drivers for the CD-ROM had to be loaded in order to load Windows 95 from the CD.

66

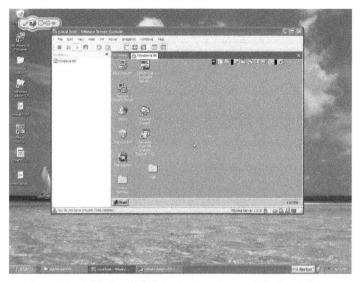

**Figure 5.2 - A Windows 95 VM guest running on a Windows XP host**

The fact that a floppy disk and a floppy disk drive is required, brings up the issue of old-hardware and media which was brought up by Mr. B. during the interview. It also points to the urgency that these O.S.' should be saved, maybe as a VM, for future recollection/use. Mr. Barhelt indicated that his agency keeps archival data for more than five years, which today, includes very old nine-track tapes for the mainframes. To read these tapes you would need nine-track tape drives, which are no longer manufactured. Fortunately, this problem will go away for organizations that only keep records for less than ten years as backup media begins to move away from magnetic media to digital media. However, organizations that keep records for much longer times might still face this unless they take actions to transfer that data from magnetic media to digital media and look at virtualizing not only the computer but the peripheral devices, like tape drives. In the old days, when hardware and hard disk storage was very expensive, tape

67

drives were used to load programs, as well as to store data. The mainframes would read data

from the magnetic tapes, process the data, and write it down to tape. Many of the initial

consumer personal computers, like the Apple and the Commodore 64, would store data to a

cassette tape drives. Eventually, these computers moved up to floppy disks and then to hard

drives. Today, if you check the Sunday newspaper adds for computers, you will be hard pressed

to find one that has a floppy disk drive. IBM started virtualizing tape drives in the 1990s

according to Bradshaw and Schroeder (2003).

**Figure 5.3 - Early laboratory prototype (a quarter-inch tape machine) of the IBM tape
drive in the Kenyon House, Poughkeepsie, New York
Source - Fifty years of IBM innovation with information storage on magnetic tape**

Once the Windows 95 was installed, the author obtained an old copy of Microsoft Office

97 and a copy of PGP version 5i from the PGP website. This version of PGP was popular in the

early 1990s. Both pieces of software installed without a hitch on the Windows 95 VM. During

the installation of PGP, the author created an encryption key pair that included his private and

public key. To test PGP encryption, the author needed a recipient encryption key, therefore,

PGP was also installed on the host XP system and encryption keys were generated under a

separate e-mail.

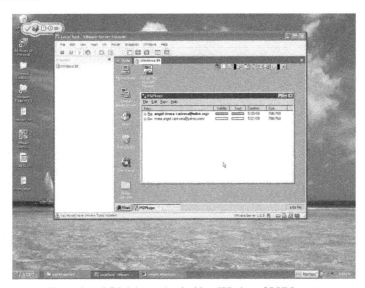

**Figure 5.4 - PGP 5.1 running inside a Windows 95 VM guest**
**The guest is running on a Windows XP host**

Once both encryption keys were created, they were saved to a floppy disk. The author

then proceeded to encrypt a text file created on Notepad with PGP. The author also created an

encrypted WordPerfect 5.0 file. This was done by creating a file in Microsoft Word-97 and then

saving the file as a WordPerfect file with password protection. When you save a file with

password protection Word will encrypt it. Once all this was done, the Windows 85 VM was

saved and copied to a DVD. The DVD also included copies of the keys and the encrypted files.

The next step was to install VMware player on a Windows Vista computer. In addition,

the latest version of PGP, PGP v8, was also installed for testing. Both products installed without a hitch.  At this point, the author was able to load the Windows 95 Image and start decrypting

and encrypting files.

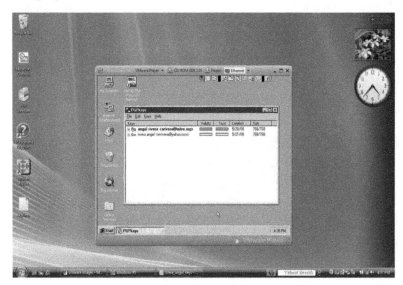

**Figure 5.5 - Windows 95 VM (with PGP) running with VM Player on a Windows Vista computer.**

The VM came up with a few errors due to the fact that the laptop running Windows Vista

did not have a floppy disk drive.  Besides the drive error at boot time, the VM worked flawlessly.

All programs including PGP, Microsoft Word, and Notepad worked. Since the keys were

available, encryption/decryption also worked well.

The last step the author took was to test for compatibility issues between legacy

applications and their newer versions.  To do this, the author attempted to decrypt a PGP 5i file

created on the Windows 95 VM. The author used PGP version 8 on the Windows Vista to do

this. As you can see in figure 5.6, the application had some problems reading the file.

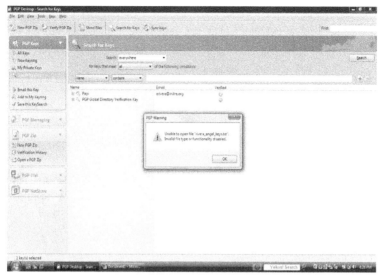

**Figure 5.6 - PGP v. 8 error message trying to read a PGP v. 5i file**

To test the encryption within Microsoft Word, and to see if the latest version of Word could still read a WordPerfect file, the author tried to open the file created on the Windows 95 VM with Microsoft Word 2007. The file was decrypted and Word had no trouble opening it.

Lessons Learned

The following bullets summarize findings and observations of the proof-of-concept:

- The process of creating VMs of old legacy operating systems and software is fairly trivial
- Obtaining legacy O.S. software and legacy hardware, like floppy disks, is becoming harder
- Legacy Encryption Software works fine inside a VM of an older O.S, as expected

71

- Leading COTS packages like Microsoft Word maintain backward compatibility for many years, in this case for more than 10 years.
- Newer Encryption Packages might have trouble reading files that have been encrypted with much older versions.
- Encryption keys/passwords must be available or the data will not be accessible
- Newer O.S.' can run legacy O.S' but this is dependent on having a VM vendor provided software like VMware Player
- VMware player needs to be installed on the host machine, it cannot run alone.

CHAPTER 6: Summary and Conclusion

Introduction

Personal and private information will continue to be stolen as long as it can be exploited

by criminals for financial gain. According to the latest Symantec Internet Security Threat Report

from April 2008, prices for credit card number are between 40 cents and twenty dollars per card.

Valid bank account numbers can fetch up to $1000. In 2006, a laptop containing personal

information on 26 million veterans was lost. This incident alone could have cost the Department

of Veterans Affairs billions of dollars, just in damage control. Encryption technology, used to

convert plain text into cipher-text, would have rendered that personal information worthless in

the black market by making it unreadable to all except the person that owns the key or the

passwords needed to covert the cipher-text into real data. By the same token, loss of the key

would mean data could be lost forever. A poorly implemented encryption strategy or having no

strategy, can easily turn into a self-inflicted denial-of-service when the organization is unable to

decrypt data. This might be because they do not have the encryption keys used to encrypt the

data in the first place.

The government, as well as corporate America, has regulatory requirements to keep

copies of electronic records for several years in case they need to be retrieved for legal or

historical purposes. However, one must ask what is the use of archiving such data if the data will

not be accessible 5-10 years from now because the software or the hardware needed to read it is

no longer available?

For libraries, the possibility of loosing digital records or access to such digital records has

been a topic of discussion for quite a while. The same applies to government agencies, since on

73

many cases, they are responsible for the preservation of critical records. In his article entitled "Ensuring the Longevity of Digital Information," Jeff Rothenberg (1999) cites a couple of cases in which digital records were lost. One well-known example was the loss of Census data from 1960. In that case, the data was lost because it was stored on digital tapes that became obsolete. Information technology systems continue to change at a very rapid pace, rendering older software and hardware obsolete or very hard to find. Electronic records are being lost daily due to the unavailability of hardware, software, or bad media.

Virtual machine software has improved substantially in the last decade to the point that it is now being installed on production environments. A recent IDC market forecast report shows a steady yearly market increase of 50%, or more, in sales and deployment of virtual machines (VM). VMs have the potential to address some of the technology challenges indentified in this paper. In particular, VMs can address legacy hardware and legacy software problems.

A key question for organizations is what happens when the records that need to be retrieved from long term storage are encrypted. Archiving data in encrypted form, which is now required by multiple regulations, presents us with multiple challenges. First, we must ensure the encryption keys used to encrypt the data are maintained and accessible. Second, we must also ensure the software used to encrypt that data is also available. Third, we must ensure the operating system and the hardware needed to read that data is available. This research attempts to answer the following key question: What is the impact of encryption on long term electronic records retention and retrieval?

The significance of this research is that it can prevent massive data losses of archival data for this generation and generations to come.

To assist in answering the key question, the research focuses on the following three sub-questions:

1. What are some of the possible consequences for organizations that are unable to retrieve encrypted records from long term storage?

2. Can encryption codes be stored for long periods of time and be linked to the encrypted records?

3. What is the current state of Virtual Computing Machines software and can this software be used to address some of the problems associated with long term archival and retrieval of encrypted records?

To complete this study, the researcher did a substantial review of literature related to the three sub-questions, and conducted interviews with industry experts, practitioners, and researchers. In addition, the researcher, as a proof-of-concept, built a portable virtual computer that was saved to a DVD and can be loaded on any current Microsoft Windows personal computer.

Summary

*What are some of the possible consequences for organization that are unable to retrieve encrypted records from long term storage?*

While the research question has the word encrypted in it, it should be noted that this section of the research was focused on the inability to retrieve any records from long term storage, not just encrypted records. A considerable amount of research is focused on establishing the value of certain data in order to establish a link between such data and the protection mechanism required by law/recommended by industry best practices. Encryption happens to be one of the most common protection mechanisms used to provide confidentiality of data.

In chapter three we start by looking at why certain data being stored on computer systems has become a target. We come to the conclusion that personal information, or PII (Personally Identifiable Information), has become lucrative target for cybercriminals. This information can be used to steal identities that can later be used to open fraudulent credit card accounts or bank accounts. In other cases, the type of PII data targeted by criminals already includes credit card numbers or bank accounts associated with an individual. This information can be used to incur in fraudulent charges on credit cards and fraudulent money transfers on bank accounts. In a few words, the incentive is money, lots of money; to the point that it is now consider part of organized crime in some countries. The chapter includes some statistical information provided by the Privacy Rights Clearing House. One statistic is that as of May 2007, the clearing house had identified data leaks incidents of at least 226,885, 128 records containing sensitive personal information (Privacy Rights Clearing House, 2007).

In this chapter we also explain the financial implications of a data leak, even if the lost or stolen data is never used for identity theft purposes. For this, we use the real case in 2006 when a laptop containing PII on 26 million veterans was stolen from a Department of Veteran Affairs employee. In this case, the Department of Veteran Affairs offered to pay credit monitoring services for all affected veterans at $75 each (Goldfard, 2006). You can do the math.

One example of a poorly thought out and deployed encryption strategy is the one being used by the Motion Picture Association of America as a copy protection mechanism. In this example, the industry revokes encryption keys that are constantly being discovered by hackers and published all over the Internet. The side effect of such a poor strategy is that older DVD

76

players cannot play the newer DVDs. So now you know why sometimes you can't play that new DVD you bought in the store today.

After establishing the value of data and the need for encryption, the author proposes three hypothetical scenarios to illustrate what could be the consequences of not being able to retrieve archival data from long term storage. The main reason for using scenarios is that it would be hard to find real examples, as most organizations would tend to keep data loss incidents under the covers. Another reason why scenarios were used was because fraud investigators and law enforcement personnel do not like to talk about fraud patterns they might be using to detect fraud.

The first scenario is about investigating tax fraud and applying a fraud pattern to multiple years worth of tax returns in order to detect possible fraud. In this scenario, the implications of not being able to retrieve records from long term storage are loss of revenue, as well as not being able to prosecute people that have committed this type of tax fraud in the past. However, the implications are far greater because this would apply to any other type of tax fraud pattern that extends multiple years. Further complicating the matter is that even if current criminals are caught, the IRS would only be able to go back 3 years and prosecute for that amount. Like many other crimes, sentencing guidelines are usually tied to the dollar amounts of the crime. The higher the dollar amount the longer the sentence.

The second scenario involves the loss of corporate data needed for a Security and Exchange Commission (SEC) investigation. This example uses a hypothetical example whereby a firm like Enron is accused of wrongdoing and the impact of not being able to access records needed to support the investigations. Ironically, during the Enron scandal, there was one instance were an e-mail was used to prove questionable accounting practices between Enron

77

Executives and Merrill Lynch Bankers. In this scenario, the impact to the investigators and prosecutors is that their case is much weaker, with less evidence. Additionally, the money trail as to where the fictitious companies were and where the funds were being transferred will probably be lost.

The third scenario revolved around drug related research data needed by a hypothetical pharmaceutical company. The scenario deals with the impact of not being able to retrieve years worth of research and a particular drug that could have benefited thousands of cancer patients. In this scenario, the loss is not only in terms of millions of research dollars but in terms of delaying a drug that has the potential of saving tenths of thousands of individuals.

To support the research included in this scenario, interviews were conducted with a computer forensic fraud investigator and an ex-chief information security officer for a pharmaceutical company.

*Can encryption codes be stored for long periods of time and be linked to the encrypted records?*

Being that more and more organizations today will be encrypting their data, this chapter explored the guidance available for handling encryption and encrypted data. The chapter also covers some examples on how some organizations and some vendors are providing tools or processes to manage encryption and encryption keys while also providing for key management and key recovery. Examples of government regulations requiring encryption of personal data and sensitive data are included in this chapter.

One example of how to manage encryption keys is to use a form of key escrow in which a third party is entrusted with maintaining track of keys and saving copies of those keys in case they are needed sometime in the future. Ironically, most of the guidance available on this topic is related to a controversial encryption computer chip called the "Clipper" chip. This chip had backdoor built in it to allow law enforcement agencies to access encryption keys used by telecommunications companies to encrypt their communications. Law enforcement agencies needed access to these keys in case they need to wiretap an encrypted telephone call. To ensure this type of wiretap was done only with court orders and proper approvals, the National Institute of Standards was tasked in 1994 with developing a key escrow standard. The politics and controversy surrounding the Clipper chip are beyond the scope of this research paper, however, the techniques and processes described in the standard should not be discounted as they can prove useful in terms of tying keys to specific encrypted information and providing for key recovery.

The Federal Government realized by the late 1990s that providing for key recovery was important, not only for law enforcement agencies, but by anyone using encryption. Realizing that there was lot of controversy surrounding the key escrow standard and the Clipper chip, NIST decided to work on a more generic type of key recovery standards. In 1998, NIST produced a proposal entitled "Requirements for Key Recovery Products." Even though the standard was never approved, the NIST document provides some very useful guidance that can be applied to key management and key recovery. Instead of specifying specific encryption chips or algorithms, the document defines an abstract model for a Key Recovery System (KRS).

One final piece of guidance that was reviewed and included in this research is NIST SP 800-57 "Recommendations for Key Management" (NIST, 2007). NIST SP 800-57 provides descriptions and processes that may be useful in addressing key management.

This chapter included an interview with an encryption expert from the Mitre Corporation and a senior IT manager for the Internal Revenue Service who was responsible for implementing tape and backup encryption for the service.

*What is the current state of Virtual Computing Machines software and can this software be used to address some of the problems associated with long term archival and retrieval of encrypted records?*

Chapter five explores the current state of virtual machine software and the market for such software. Additionally, this chapter includes the results of a proof-of-concept whereby the author attempted to create a virtual computer that is over 10 years old and no longer in use.

Virtual computing software is software that is used to emulate the hardware of an actual computer. Each emulated computer is called a virtual machine, or VM. In essence, you could have multiple VM's running in one physical computer with all the VMS sharing the hard drive, display, network interface card, etc. In Windows terms, each VM runs in a window. VMs are highly portable and not hardware dependent. The chapter describes some of the market leaders, including VMware now owned by EMC Corporation and XEN, now owned by Citrix Corporation. VMware continues to be the undisputed market leader with a majority of market share, but that market is shrinking. A version of XEN remains in the public domain and, due to the fact that it was originally freeware, it has a strong following of supporters. However, one of the disadvantages of XEN is that it only runs on Linux and not on Microsoft Windows.

Interviews with VM experts and literature review seem to indicate that VM software will eventually be free or included with most operating systems and that the market is shifting towards VM management software used to manage VMs. This shift has to do with VMs going mainstream and now being included on most large organizations strategic IT plans. The opinion of the subject matter experts, familiar with current implementations, is that most data centers today probably have VMs running in production or as a pilot. A recent market IDC VM Software

80

market forecast shows a robust virtual machine software (VMS) market growth in the past

couple of years. From 2004 to 2005 the market grew 50%, and from 2005 to 2006 the market

grew by an outstanding 69% (IDC, 2007).

The author conducted a VM proof-of-concept to demonstrate that an environment that is

14+ years old can be easily recreated today. Most government regulations require 5-10 years for

availability of the information. To do this, the author was able to build a Microsoft Windows 95

VM and encryption software from the early 1990s, as well as word processing software. The

idea behind this exercise was to simulate an environment whereby an old computer with old

encryption software could be saved as a VM and run on the latest operating system (e.g.,

Windows Vista).

One of the key findings from this proof-of concept was that the process of creating VMs

of old legacy operating systems and software is fairly trivial; however, obtaining legacy O.S.

software and legacy hardware like floppy disks is becoming increasingly harder.


Conclusion

Encryption is here to stay. Electronic records, including those containing sensitive

personal data, have become far too mobile and distributed that it would be virtually impossible to

protect all of them via physical access controls. Highly visible data breaches, like the one where

personal data for 26 million veterans was stolen, has heightened management's attention and has

resulted in a government/industry wide mandate to protect personal data. Financial implications,

not only in terms of the costs of damage-control, but in terms of legal liability, have become far

too great. However, encryption, if not properly managed, can cause data to be unreadable. The risk increases when data is encrypted and stored separate from the systems for the purposes of long-term archival storage.

Storing data off-site for the purposes of long term archival creates some interesting challenges, and encryption just adds to it. One of key challenges identified during this research were the fact that software, and maybe hardware, will be needed to retrieve and access records that have been stored away from the system for many years. The media, especially older magnetic type media, have a limited life span. Even if software and hardware is available ten years from now, and the media is readable, the encryption keys used to encrypt the data would be needed in order to decipher the data.

To address the issue of older hardware and older operating systems, as well as encryption software, virtual machines are a viable option. However, a conscious decision must be made now to preserve older hardware and older operating systems, or we run the risk of losing them forever. The possibility of data loss is also there and a comprehensive data retention strategy needs to include periodic upgrades of the storage media, periodic upgrades (if possible) to newer file formats, and frequent saving of VMs to ensure data can be retrieved and interpreted.

While encryption has become mainstream and organizations are required to encrypt records like backup and archival tapes, a comprehensive national strategy to ensure the survival of these encrypted records seems to be missing. Most organizations that use encryption today have little problem retrieving records but that is because the hardware, the software, and the keys are all available on the system. Once you decouple the data from the system, the connection between the data and all the other components is lost. What will happen ten years from today when you need to retrieve one of those records?

One of the author's incorrect assumptions when starting this research was that little guidance was available to address long-term electronic records retention, encryption key storage, and recovery. The guidance is out there, but is it so spread out that very few individuals would know where to look for it and how to put it all together. In terms of maintaining digital records accessible for many years, there is much to be learned from libraries; simply because they are dealing with the loss of massive amounts of intellectual property soon to be lost due to poor media, or lack of hardware to read the media. For key recovery and key storage, The National Institute of Standards and Technology has published a couple of standards and guidance documents. NIST has also provided guidance on Public Key Infrastructures. For government long term archival storage, the National Archives and Records Administration has provided guidance on how to store electronic records for long term storage and for how to store digital signatures and PKIs associated with certain records.

More research is needed to put all the pieces together into a comprehensive strategy for encrypted records retention. As a starting point, the strategy should consider prior work identified in this research paper. At a minimum, it should consider establishing a PKI to start managing encryption keys in an automated way. The PKI should provide for key escrow and key recovery. VMs that include hardware, encryption software, and encryption keys (protected via a key encrypting key) should also be considered. The software should be able to include an encryption key identifier field and an application identifier field on each record to ensure records are clearly associated with the application that encrypted them and the key used to encrypt them.

Lack of a comprehensive strategy can lead to the loss of valuable information, maybe forever, and the consequences can be devastating. To take lessons learned from libraries across the world, I would like to end with quote from the Task Force on Archiving of Digital

Information report published in 1996: "If we are effectively to preserve for future generations the portion of this rapidly expanding corpus of information in digital form that represents our cultural record, we need to understand the costs of doing so and we need to commit ourselves technically, legally, economically and organizationally to the full dimensions of the task. Failure to look for trusted means and methods of digital preservation will certainly exact a stiff, long-term cultural penalty" (Task Force on Archiving of Digital Information, 1996).

Appendix A:  Glossary of Acronyms and Terms


AES:  Advanced Encryption Standard

DES:  Data Encryption Standard

DEA:  Data Encryption Algorithm

TDEA:  Triple DEA

NIST:  National Institute of Standards and Technology

NIST-SP:  NIST Special Publication

NIST-FIPS:  NIST Federal Information Processing Standard

OMB:  Office of Management and Budget

PKI:  Public Key Infrastructure

VM:  Virtual Machine

Appendix B: Interview Questions

Chapter 3 Interview

*Consequences for organizations that are unable to retrieve encrypted records from long term*

*storage*

1. What is your title?

2. What kind of work do you do?

3. How many years have you been working in your field?

4. Do you have a requirement to access data from long term archival storage?

5. Is there a requirement to protect such data?

6. Can you elaborate on the types of security controls being used to protect such data?

7. Is data encryption being used or considered as a control?

8. What would be the impact of not being able to access such data?

    a. in terms of internal investigations for things like fraud?

    b. in terms of external inquiries and legal liability?

9. Are there any steps being taken to ensure such data is available when needed?

    a. periodic revalidation that old data is still accessible

10. Do you know of any cases were archived electronic records have not been accessible?

Chapter 4 Interview

*Can encryption codes be stored for long periods of time and be linked to the encrypted records?*

1. What is your title?

2. What kind of work do you do?

3. How many years have you been working in your field?

4. Does your organization use encryption?

5. For what applications? E-mail, back-up, Laptops?

6. What encryption technology and/or products do you use?

7. Do you have a PKI or similar infrastructure to manage your encryption for all applications or is it segmented by application and/or product?

8. What are your processes for Key Management?

    - How often do you change encryption keys?

    - What process do you follow to archive old keys?

9. Have you tested your key recovery capabilities?

    - DR test

    - Law enforcement inquiry

10. What would be the impact of losing archived encryption keys?

11. Do you know of any cases where archived electronic records have not been accessible?

Chapter 5 Interview:

*What is the current state of Virtual Computing Machines software and can this software be used*

*to address some of the problems associated with long term retrieval of encrypted records?*

1. What is your title?

2. What kind of work do you do?

3. How many years have you been working in your field?

4. What kind of experience do you have with virtual machine software?

5. What would you say is the current state of the VM software market?

6. Do you know of any examples of agencies that have deployed VM software and for what purposes?

5. Do you see any applications of VM software in terms of preserving legacy systems?

Appendix C:  National Institute of Standards & Technology, Computer Security Resource Center

Website

**Figure D.1 – NIST Computer Security Resource Center Website**

References

*2007 Annual Study: U.S. Enterprise Encryption Trends.* (2007, February). The Ponemon Institute, LLC.

Barker, E., Barker, W., Lee, A. (2005, December). *Guideline for Implementing Cryptography in the Federal Government.* National Institute of Standards and Technology, Special Publication 800-21. Retrieved May 15, 2008, from http://csrc.nist.gov/publications/nistpubs/800-21-1/sp800-21-1_Dec2005.pdf

Barker, E., Barker, W., Burr, W., Polk, W., & Smid, M. (2007, March). *Recommendation for Key Management (part 1).* National Institute of Standards and Technology, Special Publication 800-57. Retrieved May 4, 2008, from http://csrc.nist.gov/publications/nistpubs/800-57/sp800-57-Part1-revised2_Mar08-2007.pdf

Barker, E., Barker, W., Burr, W., Polk, W., & Smid, M. (2007, March). *Recommendation for Key Management (part 2).* National Institute of Standards and Technology, Special Publication 800-57. Retrieved May 4, 2008, from http://csrc.nist.gov/publications/nistpubs/800-57/SP800-57-Part2.pdf

Bradshaw, R., & Schroeder, C. (2003). Fifty years of IBM innovation with information storage on magnetic tape. 47(4). Retrieved May 06, 2008, from http://ed-thelen.org/1401Project/history-of-tape.pdf

A Chronology of Data Breaches. (2005, April 20). Privacy Rights Clearing House. Retrieved May 16, 2008, from http://www.privacyrights.org/ar/ChronDataBreaches.htm

Computer Security Act of 1987. Retrieved May 7, 2008, from http://www.nist.gov/cfo/legislation/Public%20Law%20100-235.pdf

Flood, M. (2004, September 21). Enron jury's told the proof is in the e-mail. *Houston Chronicle.* Retrieved May 15, 2008, from http://www.chron.com/disp/story.mpl/special/enron/barge/2807174.html

Goldfarb, Z. A. (2006, June 26). VA to Offer Credit Monitoring: 1 Year of Service Free To Data-Theft Victims. *The Washington Post.* Retrieved May 7, 2008, from http://www.washingtonpost.com/wp-dyn/content/article/2006/06/21/AR2006062101788.html

Harris, S.(2008). *All-in-one CISSP Exam Guide* (4th ed.). New York: The McGraw-Hill Companies

ID theft gang thwarts police with encryption. (2006, December 18). *CNET Networks.* Retrieved May 1, 2008, from http://www.zdnet.co.uk/misc/print/0,1000000169,39285188-39001093c,00.htm

Know Your Enemy: Honeynets. (2006, May 31). Retrieved May 9, 2008, from http://www.honeynet.org/papers/honeynet/

Lehman, K-D. (1996). Making the transitory permanent: the intellectual heritage in a digitized world of knowledge. 125(4). pp.307-329.

Lohr, S. (2007, February 27). A Software Maker Goes Up Against Microsoft. *The New York Times*. Retrieved May 28, 2008, from http://www.nytimes.com/2007/02/24/technology/24soft.html?_r=2&oref=slogin&oref=sl ogin

Lorie, R. A. (2000, May 18). *Long-Term Archiving of Digital Information*. Retrieved May 18, 2008, from http://domino.watson.ibm.com/library/CyberDig.nsf/papers/BE2A2B188544DF2C85256 90D00517082/$File/RJ10185.pdf

OMB Guidance to Federal Agencies on Data Availability and Encryption. (2006). Memorandum: M-06-16.

OMB Guidance to Federal Agencies on Data Availability and Encryption. (2006). Memorandum: M-07-16.

*Records Management Guidance For PKI-Unique Administrative Records*. (2005, March). National Archives and Records Administration. Retrieved April 29, 2008, from http://www.archives.gov/records-mgmt/faqs/pdf/final-pki-guidance.pdf
Requirements for Key Recovery Products. (1996). National Institute of Standards and Technology. Retrieved May 06, 2008, from http://csrc.nist.gov/keyrecovery/

The Research Libraries Group. (1996). *Preserving Digital Information: Report of the Task Force on Archiving of Digital Information*. Retrieved May 13, 2008, from OCLC database.

Rose, M., & Humphreys, J. (2007, August). *Worldwide Virtual Machine Software 2006 Vendor Shares*. Retrieved May 15, 2008, from IDC database.

Rose, M., & Humphreys, J. (2007, August). *Worldwide Virtual Machine Software 2007-2011 Forecast*. Retrieved May 15, 2008, from IDC database.

Ross, S., & Gow, A. (1999, February). *Digital Archaeology: Rescuing Neglected and Damaged Data Resources*. London: Library Information Technology Centre. Retrieved May 17, 2008, from http://www.ukoln.ac.uk/services/elib/papers/supporting/pdf/p2.pdf

Rothenberg, J. (n.d.). Retrieved May 1, 2008, from http://www.clir.org/pubs/reports/rothenberg/scope.html

Rothenberg, J. (1999, Feb. 22 rev.). Ensuring the Longevity of Digital Information. *Scientific American*. Retrieved May 13, 2008, from http://www.clir.org/programs/otheractiv/ensuring.pdf

RSA DES challenge broken. (1997, June 18). Retrieved June 1, 2008 from http://www2.tech.purdue.edu/cpt/courses/CPT136/desch.html

Schneier, B. (1996). *Applied Cryptography: Protocols, Algorithms, and Source Code in C* (2nd ed.). New York: John Wiley & Sons, Inc.

Semilof, M. (2006, April 3). VM market on fire with software giveaways. Retrieved May 14, 2008, from http://searchwinit.techtarget.com/news/article/0,289142,sid1_gci1177848,00.html#

Title III- Information Security. (n.d.). *National Institute of Standards and Technology*. Retrieved May 06, 2008, from http://csrc.nist.gov/drivers/documents/FISMA-final.pdf

Tulloch, M. (2003). *Microsoft Encyclopedia of Security*. (pp. 259-260)

Turner, D. (2008, April). Symantec Global Internet Security Threat Report. *Symantec, 13*. Retrieved May 02, 2008, from http://eval.symantec.com/mktginfo/enterprise/white_papers/b-whitepaper_internet_security_threat_report_xiii_04-2008.en-us.pdf

U.S. Department of Commerce. (2001, November 26). *Advanced Encryption Standard*. National Institute of Standards and Technology, FIPS 197. Retrieved May 21, 2008, from http://csrc.nist.gov/publications/fips/fips197/fips-197.pdf

U.S. Department of Commerce. (1999, October 25). *Data Encryption Standard*. National Institute of Standards and Technology, FIPS 46-3. Retrieved May 06, 2008, from http://csrc.nist.gov/publications/fips/fips46-3/fips46-3.pdf

U.S. Department of Commerce. (2000, January 27). *Digital Signature Standard*. National Institute of Standards and Technology, FIPS 186-2. Retrieved May 06, 2008, from http://csrc.nist.gov/publications/fips/fips186-2/fips186-2-change1.pdf

U.S. Department of Commerce. (2006). *Digital Signature Standard*. National Institute of Standards and Technology, FIPS 186-3. Retrieved May 06, 2008, from http://csrc.nist.gov/publications/drafts/fips_186-3/Draft-FIPS-186-3%20_March2006.pdf

U.S. Department of Commerce. (1994, February 9). *Escrowed Encryption Standard*. National Institute of Standards and Technology, FIPS 185. Retrieved May 06, 2008, from http://www.itl.nist.gov/fipspubs/fip185.htm

VA's IG Report on Stolen Laptop Puts Blame Near the Top. (2006, July). VA Watchdog. Retrieved May 17, 2008, from http://www.vawatchdog.org/old%20newsflashes%20JUL%2006/newsflash07-12-2006-7.htm

Whitehouse, L. (2006, November). Emphasis on Recovery That They Can Back Up. *Symantec*. Retrieved May 02, 2008, from http://eval.symantec.com/mktginfo/enterprise/other_resources/ent-esg_be_emphasis_on_recovery_2006.pdf

Bibliography

Ackman, D. (2004, September 20). Enron's Nigeria Barge: The Real Deal. *Forbes*. Retrieved April 28, 2008, from http://www.forbes.com/2004/09/20/cx_da_0920topnews.html

Federal Public Key Infrastructure Steering Committee Legal/Policy Working Group. (2005, March 11). *Records Management Guidance For PKI Digital Signature Authenticated and Secured Transaction Records*. National Archives and Records Administration. Retrieved April 28, 2008, from http://www.archives.gov/records-mgmt/pdf/pki.pdf

Fowler, T. (2004, October 6). Prosecutors: E-mail shows Enron deal on barges was sham. *Houston Chronicle*. Retrieved May 12, 2008, from http://www.chron.com/disp/story.mpl/special/enron/barge/ 2832680.html

Fulton, S. M. (2007, February 27). VMware: Microsoft is Rigging the Virtualization Market. *BetaNews*. Retrieved May 11, 2008, from http://www.betanews.com/article/VMware_Microsoft_is_Rigging_the_Virtualization_M arket/1172532170

History of Cryptography. (2006). Retrieved May 24, 2008, from http://www.cs.usask.ca/resources/tutorials/csconcepts/1999_3/lessons/L1/History.html#C aesar

Kelly, T. (1998). *The myth of the skytale*. Cryptologia. (pp. 244–260)

Komar, B. (2004). *Microsoft Windows Server 2003 PKI and Certificate Security*. (pp. 419-420)

Kuhn, D. R., Hu, V. C., Polk, W. T., & Chang, S.-J. (2001, February 26). *Introduction to Public Key Technology and the Federal PKI Infrastructure*. National Institute of Standards and Technology. Retrieved March 18, 2008, from http://csrc.nist.gov/publications/nistpubs/800-32/sp800-32.pdf

Kusnetzky, D. (2008). Quest Software - Embracing, extending, simplifying. *ZDNet*. Retrieved May 11, 2008, from http://blogs.zdnet.com/virtualization/?cat=3

Microsoft. (2002, June). *5-Minute Security Advisor – Recovering Encrypted Data Using EFS*, retrieved May 20, 2006, from http://www.microsoft.com/technet/archive/community/columns/security/5min/5min-401.mspx?mfr=true

Microsoft. (2005, November). *Windows XP Professional Resource Kit – Using Encrypting File System*. Retrieved May 20, 2006, from http://www.microsoft.com/technet/prodtechnol/winxppro/reskit/c18621675.mspx

*Netscape Certificate Management System Administrator's Guide: Recovering Encrypted Data.* (2000). Retrieved April 28, 2008, from http://docs.sun.com/source/816-5531-10/kycrt_ee.htm

Poulsen, K. (2008, May 13). Five IRS Employees Charged With Snooping on Tax Returns. Message posted to http://blog.wired.com/27bstroke6/2008/05/five-irs-employ.html

Public Key Cryptography (2006). *Wikipedia.* Retrieved May 12, 2008 from http://en.wikipedia.org/wiki/Public_key_encryption

Rothenberg, J. (2000, April). An Experiment in Using Emulation to Preserve Digital Publications [Electronic version]. Retrieved May 02, 2008, from http://nedlib.kb.nl/results/emulationpreservationreport.pdf

Rothenberg, J. (2000). Using Emulation to Preserve Digital Documents [Electronic version]. Retrieved May 02, 2008, from http://www.nelinet.net/edserv/conf/digital/dr_2000/rothen2.pdf

*VeriSign SSP CPS v1.0.* (2008, March 18). Retrieved May 17, 2008, from http://www.verisign.com/repository/VTN_SSP_CPS_v1.0_Final_Redacted.pdf

*Virtualization Overview.* (2006). [Pamphlet]. California: VMware Inc. Retrieved May 17, 2008, from http://www.vmware.com/pdf/virtualization.pdf

Woods, J. (2007, November 15). VMware Rules the Virtualization Market. *Seeking Alpha.* Retrieved May 11, 2008, from http://seekingalpha.com/article/54307-vmware-rules-the-virtualization-market

www.ingramcontent.com/pod-product-compliance
Lightning Source LLC
La Vergne TN
LVHW092340060326
832902LV00008B/734

* 9 7 8 3 6 6 8 0 4 9 7 2 7 *